Yearning for Eden

All the Bible Teaches About Heaven

James Allen Moseley

ISBN: 9781658222747
The Bible History Guy,
a dba of Winterwood Ministries, Inc.
(a 501(c)(3) Non-Profit Corporation)
PO Box 8
Petersham MA 01366 USA
jim@thebiblehistoryguy.com
www.thebiblehistoryguy.com
Phone: 978-456-5444
Fax: 978-234-6747

DEDICATION

To Angela, the little sister of my wife, Madlene, who
went home to be with the Lord as an infant, and to those
children of mine, who preceded me there and whom I
yearn to embrace in love.

CONTENTS

ACKNOWLEDGMENTS

Unless otherwise noted, Scripture quotations are from the Holy Bible, English Standard Version, copyright © 2001 by Crossway Bibles, a publishing ministry of Good News Publishers. Used by permission, in accordance with the "License Agreement for Bible Texts – English Standard Version," http://bibleabc.net/site/translation_esv.htm. All rights reserved or from The Holy Bible: New International Version. © 1996. Grand Rapids: Zondervan. Used in accordance with the publisher's license agreement or from original translations by the author.

WHY YOU NEED THIS BOOK

Will there be time in Heaven? Will we have bodies? Will we be young again? Is it possible to sin in Heaven? Will Heaven be boring? Will there be animals – and how about our beloved pets?

There are ten times more references in the Bible to Heaven than to Hell or Hades. By examining all the verse in Scripture about Heaven we find the Bible tells us much more about the afterlife than we often suspect. While God wants us to know that Hell is a terrifying option, He is more concerned, as a loving Father, to show what joyous rewards He has prepared for those who choose to accept Heaven through Christ. And the news is good, for the Bible also tells us precisely how know for sure that Heaven will be our eternal home.

You can know your eternal destiny for sure. The Apostle John wrote, "I write these things to you who believe in the name of the Son of God so that you may know that you have eternal life."[1]

Unfortunately, sin confuses us. "There is a way which seems right to a man, but its end is the way of death."[2]

Fortunately, the Bible makes our options clear:

"The wages of sin is death, but the gift of God is eternal life in Christ Jesus our Lord."[3]

To get to Heaven, you need to know where it is, have a passport, and you might like to be prepared for your life there.

Wouldn't it be tragic if you read this study of Heaven and did not get to go there? Wouldn't it be great if you read it and did what you need to do to know, for sure, forever, that you are going there?

WHY READ THE BIBLE?

If the Bible is a collection of moral myths, it is of some interest, but perhaps not to everyone. But if there really is a God, and if he created us with a purpose, and if he bequeathed a written record of his intentions to mankind, everyone would probably want to read it.

Many of us don't believe there really is a God, or, if we do, we simply accept the idea as inherited from others, not because we have worked the question out ourselves.

Many of us don't consider the Bible credible, like science, because we accept the prevailing superstitions of our day, thinking, as people of all ages do, that we live in an age more enlightened than others.

The great thing about the Bible is that it does not ask you to ignore doubt and take a blind leap of faith. On the contrary, Faith is the Daughter of Doubt.

God instructs us to love him with all our heart, soul, strength, and *mind*. Having endowed us with a mind, he expects us to use it in every endeavor, especially in our relationship with him. If your mind cannot find satisfactory answers about God in the Bible, you will not be able to love God intellectually or, perhaps, at all. Plato taught that we can only love that which we know.

Fortunately, this fact has not taken God by surprise. As we shall see, he embedded a wealth of intellectually satisfying answers in his Word. This book will, I hope, help you mine some of those Biblical gems.

The Bible isn't mainly about God. It isn't mainly about us. It is mainly about God's love for us and how we respond to him. However much we sin, however many Ahabs and Stalins the human race may produce, provoking the just wrath of God and man, our heavenly Father's fund of love and mercy is new every morning, yes, even to the end of the age.

DOCTRINE AND CRITICISM

No one is free of doctrinal bias. In fact, the more doctrinally biased one is, the more ardently he is likely to insist that he is only adhering to the unbiased facts. Aware that this flaw in reasoning applies to me as much as to anyone else, I have nevertheless tried to let the Bible speak for itself in matters of doctrine, rather than attempting to shoehorn the Bible into some doctrinal boot. This inevitably will arouse some objections.

In many cases variant opinions on these and other Biblical questions arise mainly because the student reads isolated passages that address a particular subject, rather than comparing all relevant passages together and reading them in a larger, fluid context. This is especially true of the Gospels, which often focus on the same subject matter but from different points of view, each adding details that amplify, refine, or clarify the meaning.

Criticism of this book is inevitable. It is also valuable, and I welcome it. I know more about the Bible today then I knew five years ago, and I expect to know more five years from now than I know today. Improving my knowledge comes largely from dealing with criticism, so it's a good thing.

I could probably have avoided a good deal of criticism if I had written this book differently. In more than 8,000 hours of primary research and teaching adult Sunday School, I have written and publicly taught through over 1,000 GB of original Bible Study Guides. These books are loaded with exegetical theses, antitheses, and footnotes. Had I included all that material in this book, it would have become much heavier reading. I might have avoided controversy with skeptics that way, but I would probably have chased away most readers. Since the aim of this book is to make the story of Jesus coherent and accessible to a wider audience, I have omitted most of the scholarly details. But they are available on my website, www.thebiblehistoryguy.com, and I am more than willing to address critique, following the maxim of the Seventeenth-Century German Lutheran theologian, Peter Meiderlin:

"In essentials, unity; in doubtful things, liberty; and in all things, charity."[4].

FORMATTING AND ERRATA

The original Bible manuscripts contain no punctuation, capital letters, or spaces between letters. To give an impression of what this looks like in Greek, handwritten before the printing press, consider John 3:16 laid out similarly in English:

Forgodsolovedtheworldthathegavehisonlysonthata llwhobelieveinhimmightnotperishbuthaveeverlasti nglife

The layout of modern Bibles is entirely a product of editorial choices. The original Gospel accounts are full of quotations and stage directions. They are dramatic. If the Bible writers had had the tools we have today, they might have written the parts of story as a stage play.

In my layout, I have often broken the paragraphs that are usually kept intact in modern printed Bibles into subparagraphs and have sometimes given separate paragraphs to lines of dialogue. Shaping the words on the page in this way, I believe, may reveal some of the Bible events as I think the authors hoped we would see them, as movies unfolding before our eyes, even as they unfolded before the gaze of eyewitnesses.

The Table of Contents in this book may not be quite exact. This is apparently a flaw in the publishing software, because although it is precise in my manuscript, some of the entries are one or more pages off after publication; but since the variance is only slight, the Table of Contents is still useful as a practical guide.

ARRIVAL IN HEAVEN

Here is a dream I once had. I cannot build doctrine on it. But its implications fascinate me. It is written in the voice of a woman I know who goes to heaven in this dream.

I looked into my husband's eyes for the last time. They were full of tears. I felt his hand caress my cheek. I heard his voice catch with emotion as he whispered, "I will always love you."

I hadn't the strength to answer. I smiled and nodded. My eyes replied, "I will always love you."

My eyelids felt so heavy – with a sleep deeper than I'd ever known. They closed.

And then he was gone. Or, rather, I was gone.

My eyes fluttered open again, taking no longer than usual. But I gasped as clean, cool, fresh air rushed through my lungs. It was like the air behind a waterfall, or in a pine forest just below the timberline, or on a tropical beach – all those aromas and feelings at once. I never tasted such delicious air. I sat up, startled.

My limbs were light. My whole body was light. I stood, effortlessly. Behind me was the edge of a forest. A broad meadow stretched out before me, rising to a beautiful hilltop. The breeze rippled the blue-green grass, stroking it with golden sunlight, as if with the brush of an invisible painter.

The blood rushed to my head. I was happy. Happy the way a beautiful spring day makes the heart soar. Happy the way you feel seeing crimson and yellow autumn leaves against an azure sky. Happy the way the first snowfall makes children and puppies frolic and squeal.

Then I heard someone speak my name.

1

"Madlene. You're here at last."

I turned and saw a young woman, in her twenties. She was exquisite: slim, shapely, with dark, wavy hair and the dancing brown eyes of a gazelle. She was familiar. My heart felt a pang.

"Don't you know me?" she smiled.

"No," I answered. I was startled again. My voice – it was my voice, but it sounded so young, so sweet, like the chime of a silver bell. "No, I'm sorry," I said, partly to be polite, partly to experience the new feeling of my voice again.

"I'm Angela," she said, softly.

It took me a moment. My little sister had died as an infant. I remembered her. I had cradled her in my arms. But I hadn't thought of her for eighty years. Now emotions I could hardly understand flooded my heart and mind. I cried. But I wasn't sad.

She came close to me and embraced me. I looked up. Our eyes met. I frowned. This was a twenty-year-old woman, not my baby sister. She laughed.

"You don't believe me. All right, watch."

She stepped backwards and, smiling, raised her hand above her head. Then her palm drifted across her face, down her neck, across her chest, waist, and down to her thighs. As her hand passed over her body, it seemed to waver, like a mirage, shimmer, and transform. Instantly, before me, I saw the little baby girl that I remembered from so long ago. The baby spoke, as the adult she had been a moment before.

"Now do you remember? This is what I looked like then."

I was too astonished to speak. She laughed.

"Would you like to hold me again?"

Instinctively, awe-struck, I picked her up. She was so light, so lovely. I stroked her soft brow. My tears dropped on her cheeks and, smiling, she wiped them away with a chubby hand. I stood a few moments in silent wonder. Then I felt a finger, gentle as velvet, wipe the tears from *my* cheek. Again, I startled, and wheeled around, holding Angela protectively.

There was a Man, tall, smiling, whose eyes were filled with light. I noticed at once the hand with which He had so tenderly wiped away my tear – the wrist bore a wound, neither healed nor bleeding, a piercing gash as if from a nail. I understood. I could say nothing.

"Please put me down now," said Angela.

Overwhelmed, I laid her gently in the grass. In an instant, she resumed her twenty-year-old form.

"Have you shown Madlene how beautiful she is today?" asked the Man, turning to Angela.

"Not yet," she grinned.

"Well, show her, and then take her to see your parents and your grandparents. You know how impatient they have been."

"Come on," said my sister.

But I couldn't move. I just gazed at the Man. I couldn't take my eyes off Him. I couldn't take my mind or heart off Him. He was so wonderful, like the sun, the moon, and everything I had ever loved throughout my life. I ached to bring my husband and children here to see Him, to be by my side in His presence.

"They will come, in the perfect time," smiled the Man, reading my mind. "Now, go with your sister. Go see your reflection in the brook over there," He said, pointing to a stream nearby. "I want you to enjoy how beautiful you are today and will always be and always were in the mind of my Father and our Spirit and Me. We will have plenty of time together. Right now, you have thousands of people to see and a whole new world to explore."

And He was gone.

A GLIMPSE OF HEAVEN

There are ten times more references in the Bible to Heaven than to Hell or Hades. While God wants us to know that Hell is a terrifying option, He is more concerned, as a loving Father, to show what joyous rewards He has prepared for those who choose to accept Heaven through Christ.

With no disrespect to John Newton's wonderful hymn, *Amazing Grace,* are these sketches of Heaven contradictory? Which sees the full picture of Heaven better?

> *When we've been there ten thousand years*
> *Bright shining as the sun.*
> *We've no less days to sing God's praise*
> *Than when we've first begun.*

Or

> *Heaven, I'm in heaven,*
> *And my heart beats so that I can hardly speak*
> *And I seem to find the happiness I seek*
> *When we're out together dancing cheek to cheek.*
>
> *Oh, I love to climb a mountain*
> *And reach the highest peak*
> *But it doesn't thrill me half as much*
> *As dancing cheek to cheek.*
>
> *Heaven, I'm in heaven*
> *And my heart beats so that I can hardly speak,*
> *And I seem to find the happiness I seek,*
> *When we're out together dancing cheek to cheek.*

The truth is, there's reality in both – for the rapture of adoring God's awesome presence and for dancing, mountain-climbing, fishing, and feeling heart-thrilling happiness in Heaven.

While the prospect of Hell is terrifying, Heaven is much more than a mere escape from Hell.

Heaven is the greatest good, the highest happiness, that we ever have experienced on earth, taken beyond the limits of our imagination.

The best of Earth is a glimpse of what Heaven is like. The worst of Earth is a glimpse of what Hell is like.

COMMON BELIEFS ABOUT HEAVEN

Most civilizations, from prehistory until now, have believed in some form of afterlife.

Hindus and Buddhists believe that they are reincarnated according to their deeds. If they do bad deeds, they come back as inferior beings, possibly as animals. A flea who behaves well, on the other hand, may come back as a human. The final achievement is Nirvana – unity with God (Brahman) – which means not coming back at all.

Muslims believe that Allah judges souls according to their deeds. Those who confess that Muhammad is God's prophet and have followed God's commands may, after death, cross the knife-edged bridge to Paradise or fall into the consuming flames of Hell. Their eternal destiny becomes clear only on the Day of Judgment. Martyrs in Holy War (*jihad*) are an exception. They go straight to Paradise. This is why jihad attracts tormented people – in Islam it is supposedly the *only* way of knowing for certain where they will go after death. (Paradise, by the way, is an ancient Persian word that means "enclosure" or "park." Translated into Greek, it came to designate the Garden of Eden. It is not originally a Biblical word.)

Jews believe that God accepts them into Heaven based on how well they have observed the Law of Moses – even though key parts of the law, such as bringing sacrifices to the Temple on the Day of Atonement, have been impossible since Rome destroyed Jerusalem in A.D. 70. I have a Jewish rabbi friend who believes that even Hell observes the Sabbath – that its tormenting flames are extinguished every Saturday so as not to violate the Fourth Commandment.

Atheists believe that the end of life is the end of consciousness.

Many Christians believe (incorrectly) they will go to Heaven because they attend church regularly or do good deeds.

The Bible, which is our only credible guide, nowhere promises that anyone can earn a ticket to Heaven. It is, rather, the free gift of God to any who chose to believe and accept it.

Does everyone believe in any one thing? Yes. Everyone believes in death. The death rate is one per person. No one gets out of this life alive.

A ROAD MAP TO HEAVEN

To get to Florida, you have to know where Florida is, and you need an airplane, train, bus ticket, a license to drive or sneakers and a map.

If you plan to stay in Florida for a while, you might like to pack a swim suit and a snorkel, not snowshoes or ice skates.

To get to Heaven, you need to know where it is, have a passport, and you might like to be prepared for your life there.

Early Christian martyrs, who entered Heaven through public torture in Nero's gardens or by facing the lion's gory mane, survived those torments because they had a clear vision of their eternal destiny. They sang hymns of joy as they felt their flesh burn or felt their limbs torn and their bones crack. The catacombs of Rome show ancient graffiti like: "In Christ, Alexander is not dead, but lives."

THE PAIN OR THE PEACE OF DEATH?

Could you know this kind of peace if you were saved in Christ? Or is this just the stuff of legends? Or were these early Christians mind-numbed fanatics?

In 1884, a lion attached David Livingstone, the physician, Christian missionary and African explorer.

"I heard a shout. Starting and looking half around, I saw the lion just in the act of springing upon me. I was on a little height; he caught my shoulder as he sprang and we both came to the ground below together. Growling horribly close to my ear, he shook me as a terrier does a rat. The shock produced a stupor similar to that which seems to be felt by a mouse after the first shake by a cat. It caused a sort of dreaminess in which there was no sense of pain or feeling of terror, though quite conscious of all that was happening. It was like what patients partially under the influence of chloroform describe, who see all the operation but feel not the knife. This singular condition was not the result of any mental process. The shake annihilated fear and allowed no sense of horror in looking around at the beast. The peculiar state is probably produced in all animals killed by carnivora; and if so, is a merciful provision by our benevolent Creator for lessening the pain of death."

One of Livingstone's companions fired a shotgun at the lion and missed but succeeded in scaring the lion away. So, Livingstone survived, but let's pay close attention to these words from a man who came close to dying in a way similar to the persecuted Christians in Nero's arena.

His peaceful state of mind seemed "a merciful provision by our benevolent Creator for lessening the pain of death."

God knows that we all must pass through the door of death. He has good reasons for making this our escape hatch from a fallen world. And, as a loving Father, He has the will and the power to make that final passage a peaceful one – for "we know that for those who love God all things work together for good, for those who are called according to his purpose."[5] Even death.

HEAVEN'S LOCATION

Skeptics say that when Jesus ascended to Heaven and disappeared from the Apostles' sight, even if He traveled at the speed of light, He still would be traveling through our galaxy and would not have reached Heaven even today. Of course, Jesus' Ascension does not mean merely that He went up. He transcended time and space.

Heaven is a dimension outside the dimensions we inhabit on this earth. Jesus' ability to appear and disappear after the Resurrection – His ability to step in and out of time and space as we step in and out of a river – gives a glimpse of Heaven's metaphysical reality.

Jesus said, "In My Father's house are many dwelling places; if it were not so, I would have told you; for I go to prepare a place for you. If I go and prepare a place for you, I will come again and receive you to Myself, that where I am, you may be also. And you know the way where I am going."

Thomas, blunt as ever, replied: "Lord, we do not know where you are going. How do we know the way?"

Jesus said to him, "I am the way, and the truth, and the life; no one comes to the Father but through Me."[6]

So, Heaven is both a place and a relationship.

Paul wrote: "For me, to live is Christ and to die is gain[7]...I am hard-pressed from both directions, having the desire to depart and be with Christ, for that is very much better[8]...while we are at home in the body we are absent from the Lord[9]...we...prefer rather to be absent from the body and at home with the Lord."[10]

Revelation describes the physical and relational aspects of our final destination.

"Then I saw a new heaven and a new earth; for the first heaven and the first earth passed away, and there is no longer any sea.

"And I saw the holy city, New Jerusalem, coming down out of heaven from God, made ready as a bride adorned for her husband.

"And I heard a loud voice from the throne, saying, 'Behold, the tabernacle of God is among men, and He will dwell among them, and they shall be His people, and God Himself will be among them, and He will wipe away every tear from their eyes; and there will no longer be any death; there will no longer be any mourning, or crying, or pain; the first things have passed away.'

"And He who sits on the throne said, "Behold, I am making all things new."[11]

Heaven is where we go to be with Christ; yet in another sense, Christ is the fulfillment of the Promised Land. In Jesus, Paradise Lost becomes Paradise Restored.

GOD'S PLAN FOR OUR FUTURE

Many people think Heaven is eternal tedium – one unending church service, hymn after hymn, sermon after sermon, forevermore, amen.

But the Apostle Paul wrote:

"...[the] eye has not seen and ear has not heard, and [they] have not entered the heart of man, all that God has prepared for those who love Him."[12]

This might seem to suggest that we cannot know much about Heaven. But we can; the next verse in this passage makes the *opposite* point:

"For to us God revealed them through the Spirit; for the Spirit searches all things, even the depths of God."[13]

The New Testament has 248 references to Heaven and 23 references to Hades or Hell. If God did not intend for us to know a great deal about Heaven, He wouldn't have revealed so much to us in Scripture. By dredging the Bible for clues, we can come up with an extensive picture of what Heaven is like.

Also, God clearly intends to entice us more with the rewards of Heaven than to threaten us with the terrors of Hell. God made us to desire and enjoy just rewards. He wants us to know how bad an option Hell is; but as a loving Father, He wants even more for us to realize what an appealing future Heaven is.

Heaven is where God *wants* us to go. Jesus said that God is not willing that even one soul should be lost and that there is there is "joy in the presence of the angels of God over one sinner who repents."[14]

We don't wish for Heaven because it's a pleasant fantasy. We desire it because it is a future that really exists and for which God created us. We are wired for Heaven, not Hell. We "desire a better country, a heavenly one."[15] In fact, Scripture commands us to set our "hearts on things above, where Christ is seated at the right hand of God."[16]

SATAN'S PLAN FOR OUR FUTURE

Satan is our enemy and a liar.

"When he lies, he speaks his native language, for he is a liar and the father of lies."[17]

Satan curses God, Heaven, and all who live in Heaven.[18] He does this because God expelled Satan from Heaven.

One of Satan's shrewdest lies is to persuade us that Heaven isn't worth having, that it's boring, that those who go there will have to give up the things they really love and desire most on Earth.

THE TRUTH ABOUT HEAVEN

Heaven not only embodies the best of what we love about this Earth, it improves upon it. Revelation 21 teaches us that:

1. A new Earth will replace this one.
2. The new Earth will be better.
3. God and people will live as Father and children.
4. Pain, tears, and death are temporary; they will have no place in Heaven.
5. All things will be made new – not *some* things – *all*.
6. We can trust this promise.
7. Anyone who desires this promise can have it.
8. Anyone who rejects it will perish.

GOING TO HELL

Two people die every second, 15 every minute, and over 6,000 every hour.[19] More than 150,000 people every day go to Heaven or Hell.

The question is where are most of us going? Heaven or Hell?

Seventy-five percent of Americans think they are going to Heaven.[20] The truth is the reverse. Most of humanity from all history is going to Hell. How do we know?

Jesus said, "Wide is the gate and broad is the road that leads to destruction, and many enter through it. But small is the gate and narrow the road that leads to life, and only a few find it."[21]

Since "all have sinned and fall short of the glory of God,"[22] Heaven is no longer, after the Fall, our *default* destiny. Hell is. Sin separates us from God,[23] because God's "...eyes are too pure to look on evil; [He] cannot tolerate wrong."[24]

Only those whose names are written in the Book of Life will enter Heaven.[25] Our lives may end at any second. In a parable, Jesus related how God told a rich man, "You fool! This very night your soul is required of you; and now who will own what you have prepared?"[26]

The author of Hebrews wrote, "It is appointed for men to die once and after this comes judgment."[27]

JUDGMENT

Jesus told us what will happen in the Final Judgment:

"Do not marvel at this; for an hour is coming, in which all who are in the tombs will hear His voice and will come forth; those who did the good *deeds* to a resurrection of life, those who committed the evil *deeds* to a resurrection of judgment."[28]

In other words, without help – salvation by God – every one of us will be judged with perfect justice according every one of our deeds, everything done publicly and in secret, all summed up, all exposed in brutal, harsh, uncompromising honesty. How many of us are really confident that a jury of our peers – let alone God – would acquit and send us to Heaven if they knew all?

Christ will say to those not found in the Lamb's Book of Life, those who are not covered by His grace, "Depart from me, you who are cursed, into the eternal fire prepared for the devil and his angels."[29]

What Hell is Like

Jesus described Hell as a real and appalling place. He said it is a place

- where both body and soul are destroyed,[30]
- of outer darkness,[31]
- of weeping and gnashing teeth,[32]
- where the worm does not die, and the fire is unquenched.[33]

In the story of the wicked man and Lazarus,[34] Jesus illustrated that the condemned

- suffer terribly,
- are conscious,

- retain their desires, memories, and reasoning,
- yearn for relief,
- cannot be comforted,
- cannot leave their torment, and
- have no hope.

Heaven is a place of joy, companionship, pleasure, creativity, achievement, activity, sport, freedom, spiritual and mental challenge and growth.

Hell is a place of sorrow, loneliness, pain, boredom, insignificance, inactivity, imprisonment, regret and despair. Hell is the absence of all good. It is the absence of God.

Hell will last enduringly. Jesus says that some will "go away to eternal punishment, but the righteous to eternal life."[35]

Paul says of those who die without Jesus, "They will be punished with everlasting destruction and shut out from the presence of the Lord and from the majesty of His power." Hell is the greatest tragedy in the universe.

People lightly say, "Go to Hell," as if that required any special effort. Actually, most people already are set on autopilot for Hell. A change of course requires a change of heart.

Is Hell Forever?
This depends on what two words in the Bible mean – "eternal" and "perish." Let's examine these and see what emerges.

Eternal
In the New Testament, the word for eternal is αἰώνιος, *aiónios*. This Greek word derives from αἰών, *aión* (English eon), which means "age" or "duration of time."

In Matthew 12:32, Jesus says:

"And whoever speaks a word against the Son of Man will be forgiven, but whoever speaks against the Holy Spirit will not be forgiven, either in this age (eon) or in the age (eon) to come."

These phrases are similar in Hebrew.

The word עוֹלָם, *olam*, means "age."

HaOlam HaZeh means "the age that is."

HaOlam HaBa means "the age to come."

Loosely, these terms mean "this world" and "the next world."

Jesus, the second man in history to be called a rabbi (after John the Baptist), was perfectly attuned to the Hebrew views about "this world and the next" that prevailed in his day – and that would prevail in the Mishnah, the Jewish "oral Torah," compiled by Yehudah haNasi (Judah the Prince; c. 165-220 A.D.).

Here's an example of the word *olam* in Genesis 9:12 (literally translated):

"And God said, 'This is the token of the covenant which I make between you and between me and between every living creature that is with you, unto age-long generations (*olam*).'"

The Bible tells us that this age will end (2 Peter 3:10). Therefore, God's rainbow covenant is not perpetual in the sense of being never-ending, but it is "*olam*" in the sense of lasting as long as this age does.

Our English word, eternal, derives from Latin *aeternus*, which derives from *aevum*, which also means "age."

All these words therefore mean "age-long." They do not necessarily mean "everlasting" or "never-ending."

When Jesus says He will be with us till the end of the age (*aión*), he does not mean he will *not* be with us *after* the end of the age. But he will be with us all along our journey through *this* age, which is a finite journey.

So, the Biblical words often translated as "never-ending" or "everlasting" actually mean "age-enduring."

They *may* also, in context, mean "never-ending." But they may also, in context, mean "lasting as long as an age."

To understand the Bible reverently and accurately, we should prayerfully consider the *context* in which God places these words.

Perish

In New Testament Greek, this word perish is ἀπόλλυμι or *apóllimi*, which means to kill, destroy, die, or pass away.[36]

In Old Testament Hebrew, this word is אָבַד or *abad*, which means annihilate, be lost, broken, corrupts, destroy, die, obliterate, perish, ruin, waste, or wipe.[37]

The word perish is not so difficult to understand. It just means to die or cease to exist.

The thought-provoking Biblical idea is the contrast of "perish" with "eternal life." The Bible seems to suggest that eternal life equals not perishing. So eternal life seems never to end, but perishing, the alternative, is a definitive end.

This suggests that the saved never cease to exist but that the unsaved do cease to exist. However, it does not explain exactly *when* they cease to exist. The Bible definitely states that perishing does not equal escape from punishment, for example, in Hell.

Key examples of its Biblical use are:

For God so loved the world, that he gave his only Son, that whoever believes in him should not *perish* but have eternal life.[38]

I give them eternal life, and they will never *perish*, and no one will snatch them out of my hand.[39]

No, I tell you; but unless you repent, you will all likewise *perish*.[40]

For all who have sinned without the law will also *perish* without the law, and all who have sinned under the law will be judged by the law.[41]

Is Hell Fair?

One objection many have to Christian doctrine is whether the concept of eternal – never-ending – torment as punishment in Hell is fair. If a person sinned for 90 years, would it make sense for God to pour wrath on him for millions – or infinite – years?

Or would it make more sense for God to punish worse sinners longer and lesser sinners for a shorter time? This is controversial, but it is a possible interpretation of the Bible that many orthodox Christian scholars have, indeed, held. So, before your blood pressure rises, please just consider it as a possible – but not necessarily true – doctrine.

Take this example: your local spinster librarian (if unsaved) may be a sinner who will go to Hell – but is it really just to punish her to the same degree as to punish Stalin, the murder of 20 million people?

Perhaps it is, but it is possible, from reading the Bible, to deduce that this may not be the way God executes justice.

What may happen in Hell is that sinners may suffer torment – which is conscious isolation apart from God – for some period of time, but not forever. Possibly people who have worked extraordinary evil in their lifetimes suffer longer, and people who have done less evil suffer for a shorter time. And possibly at the end of a just sentence of punishment, these lost souls perish – meaning they expire or cease to exist. How? God may cease to inspire them – breathe His Spirit into them – and without that animating energy, those souls die.

This may contrast with souls in Heaven that God continuously inspires – breathes His Spirit into – allows to drink rivers of living water forever; those souls never die. The intriguing thing about this view is that the Bible is unambiguous about salvation lasting forever. So everlasting life is a promise with no expiration date.

Again, it is plausible to reject this doctrine by interpreting the Bible differently – that is it may be true that Hell is a place where the torment never ends. The best argument in favor of this is Jesus' statement that Hell is a place "where the worm does not die, and the fire is unquenched."[42]

But a possible counterargument is that just because the worm and the fire do not die does not mean the souls upon whom they act do not perish.

Why does this matter?

Well, if you're a person who says, "I just can't believe in a God who would execute never-ending punishment on people in Hell," now you can accept God and go to Heaven. This is a reading of Scripture that is fair and within the pale of orthodoxy and removes your "reason" for not going to Heaven.

And whether Hell is a place where you suffer torment as punishment for a few decades or forever, it's definitely not some place you want to go. Because it and its suffering are real. Much better to go to Heaven. Everlasting life is far preferable to painful punishment, of any duration.

God's Feelings about Hell

God wants no one to go to Hell. That's why He tells us the truth about Hell in the Bible.

But if God is omnipotent and good, why doesn't He just save everybody?

He did. Everyone on earth is potentially saved. "God so loved the world that He sent His only Son, that *all* who believe in Him might not perish, but have everlasting life."

Christ's offer stands. But most people refuse to accept the free gift.

God is not a cosmic rapist, meaning He will not *force* us to love him.

And He is not a cosmic puppeteer, giving us no *choice* but to love Him.

He gives us free will – the potential to love or reject Him.

Heaven or Hell is merely the ratification of our free choice on Earth.

Jesus came to seek the lost, to die for them, and to offer them the free gift of salvation. This is called "grace." All we have to do is RSVP.

Grace

The word for grace in New Testament Greek is χάρις, *cháris*[43] (a feminine noun from *xar-*, "favor, disposed to, inclined, favorable towards, leaning towards to share benefit). *Cháris* is used of the Lord's favor – freely extended to give himself away to people (because he is "always leaning toward them").

Cháris ("grace") answers directly to the Hebrew (OT) term *Kaná*[44] ("grace, extension-toward").

Both words refer to God freely extending himself (his favor, grace), reaching (inclining) to people because he is disposed to bless (be near) them.

Cháris is sometimes rendered "thanks;" the expression "thank you" in Spanish is *gracias* and in Italian it is *grazie* – "graces," or reaching out in gratitude for a favor granted.

Thus, grace is the act of God doing man a favor or kindness by reaching out to him.

A good depiction of grace is Jesus extending his hand to Peter and lifting him, as Peter was sinking beneath the stormy waves on the Sea of Galilee.

Passport from Hell

Jesus said, "No one comes to the Father except through me."[45] It is fashionable to say that there are as many paths to God as there are hearts to men. Unfortunately, that is untrue. There is only one road: through Christ. Jesus came to deliver us from death. The author of Hebrews wrote:

Therefore, since the children share in □□□□flesh and blood, □□He Himself likewise also partook of the same, that □□through death He might render powerless □□him who had the power of death, that is, the devil, and might free those who through □□fear of death were subject to slavery all their lives.[46]

Because he was sure of the promise of resurrection, Paul wrote: "O Death, where is your victory? O Death, where is your sting?"[47]

THE DOCTRINE OF ORIGINAL SIN

Is this doctrine fair? Is it just a propagandistic myth designed to scare people into Christianity – or does it have the support of empirical, scientific observation?

Adam's sin brought death not only to Adam and Eve, but also to all their descendants and to the earth itself. How could this be? Possibly God activated the phenomenon of entropy (Newton's Second Law of Thermodynamics) at the time He banished the first humans from Eden. That would explain the steady decay not only of human bodies but also of the cosmos and would validate the comparison of earth's current Fallen State to its former state of deathless innocence in Eden.

If true, this would mean that this universal law had a starting point *after* the creation of the universe. While God states the order in which He created some things, like plants, birds, and man, He does not tell us that He absolutely created every law of physics at the same time that He created matter and energy and time. Much as we might wish to deduce that He did so – and even argue for the necessity of it – He is not obliged to fit our conception of what is possible or not. Science makes an assumption here and an assumption there and comes up with a number. Fine. But it is risky to try to back the Bible into equations so formulated, when the record of science is one of constantly *changing* assumptions. Galileo sad the Bible tells us how to go to heaven, not how the heavens go.

The overriding point is this: no matter how brilliant man becomes, it is philosophically certain that God's mind and power will always present elements of mystery to the human intellect. Attempts to reduce the Bible – or Nature – to the point that they conform perfectly to human rationale and contain no element of mystery are philosophically absurd. God made the world as He wished to make it and left us the record He wished us to have of it.

It is intriguing to debate secondary issues, such as the age of the earth, but the essential truth is that God is the sovereign First Cause, man sinned and fell short of God's plan, and God provided a new plan with fixed rules that invite mortal mankind to redemption and eternal life in Christ.

The Fall

In Genesis 2, God created Eden, a perfect habitat for Adam, where God and man could commune. Then God created the first woman, Eve, as Adam's companion. And then came the famous story of original sin – the Fall.

The Key Points of the Story

God gave Adam the gift of working the garden before sin entered the world. Work is not a curse. It is a blessing. God works, and He never ceases to work.

In John 5:17, Jesus says, "Until now My Father is working, and I too am working."

Psalm 147:9 says, "He gives to the beasts their food, and to the young ravens that cry."

Psalm 104 says: all creatures "look to you, to give them their food in due season. When you give it to them, they gather it up; when you open your hand, they are filled with good things. When you hide your face, they are dismayed; when you take away their breath, they die and return to their dust.

When you send forth your Spirit, they are created, and you renew the face of the ground."

Acts 17:28 says, "In him we live and move and have our being."

So, God *always* works – if He ceased working, the universe would collapse. Even on the Seventh Day following Creation, God worked – He just stopped the *specific* work of Creation, but He continued the *general* work of sustaining His Creation. Work is a pleasure for God, and He made our work to be a blessing for us.

But after the Fall, God cursed the ground (but not humanity), and because of this, Adam's working it would no longer be an unalloyed joy; since the ground would no longer be perfect, working it would become difficult, painful, and tiring.

As God made labor in the field painful, he also made labor in childbearing painful. What, presumably, would have been without pain in sinless Eden became a source of pain and fatigue in the fallen world.

God cursed the serpent, as well as all the other animals, for they, too, became subject to aging and death. God did not say that other animals would *not* be cursed, but that the serpent would be cursed even *more* than they were.

The serpent is, of course, a guise of Satan, the tempter and enemy of God and man. The Genesis account probably means to say not that Satan *was* a serpent, but that Satan was *like* a serpent or spoke *through* a serpent, as a ventriloquist speaks though his dummy.

God promised that there would be, someday, a significant struggle between a human and Satan. This particular human – one man, for the Bible says "he" not "they" – would prevail over Satan, for he would wound Satan's head, while Satan would only wound his heel. That is, Satan's injury of the man would be a setback. The man's injury of Satan would be a victory.

God's Choices

When Adam and Eve sinned, God had several choices. He could have:

1. Overlooked their sin and have pretended nothing had happened.
2. Scrapped Adam, Eve, and the world and have started all over.
3. Laid a plan to redeem Adam and Eve.

The Bible obviously attests that God took the third way. That is what all of Scripture is about. But were the first two options realistic? Let's consider them.

The sin of Adam and Eve did not hurt God. He is entirely whole and self-sufficient. No one can hurt Him. He can feel deep compassion for his creatures, but that's different from being wounded personally.

But the sin of Adam and Eve profoundly wounded Adam and Eve. They immediately and permanently changed. They were ashamed, not simply of failing God's trust, but even of their own skins. God would have to be a cold, unloving Father to leave them in that cowering confused state.

He could have destroyed them in righteous anger or pity. They had tracked mud into His perfect world. Surely, it would not have been too hard for God to make the world again from scratch. It is not as though He had too little time or energy. He is the author of both time and energy. He has all of them that He wants. So, what stopped Him from starting

all over again? Obviously, as disappointing as
Adam and Eve were, God must have loved them
personally. They were not mere toys to him. As a
loving, sympathetic Father, God demanded that
Adam and Eve be honest with Him and with
themselves. He explained the consequences they
faced and gave them His plan – one with a future
and a hope.[48]

Mortal Life Instead of Immortal Death

When man sinned, God barred man from Eden
specifically so that he might not eat of the Tree of
Life and live forever. This was mercy, for otherwise
man would have lived forever in a state of sin. He
would be immortally sinful. Romans 6:23 tells us
"the wages of sin are death, but the free gift of God
is eternal life in Christ Jesus our Lord."

If Adam and Eve ate the fruit of the tree of life,
sinfulness would have become immortal, and
consequently death would have become immortal.
They would have "lived" forever in a state of
"death."

God instead introduced mortality, the merciful
end of man's sinful state through the portal of
physical death. That is, death became the doorway
of release from a painful life of constant sinning.

Can Man's Sin Produce a Curse on Nature?

The cause of evil is the sin of *man*. The evil done by
men is a result of their free will. The cure – entropy
– death – must, by definition, permit evil to a point,
as long as God permits man to live.

The destabilization of Nature caused by sin –
entropy – may be the cause of natural disasters.

Romans 8:22 says, "For we know that the whole creation has been groaning together in the pains of childbirth until now."

Bad things – like earthquakes and floods – do not just "happen" to "good" people. Rather, there are really no "good" people – all sin and fall short of the glory of God – and entropy – the decay that leads from a perfectly ordered world to an increasingly chaotic one – may be both the consequence of and the antidote to humanity's original and ongoing sinful behavior.

WHY DOES GOD PERMIT EVIL?

God could remove evil from the world in one of three ways:

1. He could take away man's free will. This would reduce us to slavery. Yet we instinctively rebel against slavery, even if we are the slaves of virtue. We instinctively cherish free will, even with its risks. This is an indicator that free will is an innately good gift from God.
2. He could remove all sinful mankind from the world, starting with you and me.
3. He could destroy and re-create the world.

Time is what keeps everything from happening at once, and the Bible teaches that God does plan to adopt all three options, but each in its proper time.

God plans to preserve man in a state of free will; this *allows* evil to occur, but it does not *force* evil to occur – it allows man to accept God's guidance and choose what is good.

And God does plan to remove all mankind from the world at the final resurrection. But he loves all his human creatures enough to offer them each, personally, the chance – through free will – to accept His gift of grace and salvation through Jesus.

And He does in fact plan to make a new creation in which will dwell righteousness where God will again live in direct fellowship with regenerate mankind – at the end of time. The Bible describes this fully in Revelation 21 and 22, as follows.

The End of Sin

"Then I saw a new heaven and a new earth, for the first heaven and the first earth had passed away, and the sea was no more.

"And I saw the holy city, New Jerusalem, coming down out of heaven from God, prepared as a bride adorned for her husband.

"And I heard a loud voice from the throne saying, "Behold, the dwelling place of God is with man. He will dwell with them, and they will be his people, and God himself will be with them as their God.

"He will wipe away every tear from their eyes, and death shall be no more, neither shall there be mourning, nor crying, nor pain anymore, for the former things have passed away."[49]

"Then the angel showed me the river of the water of life, bright as crystal, flowing from the throne of God and of the Lamb through the middle of the street of the city; also, on either side of the river, the tree of life with its twelve kinds of fruit, yielding its fruit each month. The leaves of the tree were for the healing of the nations.

"No longer will there be anything accursed, but the throne of God and of the Lamb will be in it, and his servants will worship him.

"They will see his face, and his name will be on their foreheads. And night will be no more. They will need no light of lamp or sun, for the Lord God will be their light, and they will reign forever and ever."[50]

SOUL AND SPIRIT

We often use the word soul and spirit interchangeably, but the Bible makes a clear distinction between them, as in this verse:

"For the word of God is living and active, sharper than any two-edged sword, piercing *to the division of soul and of spirit,* of joints and of marrow, and discerning the thoughts and intentions of the heart."[51]

From this passage we can see the following dichotomies in the human make-up:

1. Soul vs. spirit
2. Joints vs. marrow
3. Thoughts vs. intentions of the heart

Since God's word can divide the soul (Greek ψυχή, *psyché*, meaning soul, life, or self) from the spirit (Greek πνεῦμα, *pneúma*, meaning wind, breath, or spirit), the soul and the spirit are not the same thing. The same thing cannot be divided from itself. However, soul and spirit are both part of each human being.

Similarly, joints are not the same thing as marrow, but they are both part of the human physical body, which is integral to the identity of each human being.

Similarly, thoughts are not the same as feelings (intentions of the heart), but every human has both.

In English, spirit comes from the Latin word, *spiritus,* which means "breath." The Latin word for soul is *animus,* which is where we derive the word animals – for creatures with souls (as opposed, for example, to trees).

The Bible's term for the Holy Spirit in Greek is Πνεῦμα Ἅγιον, *Pneuma Agion,* or "Holy Breath."

Why would the third Person of the Trinity be the "breath" of God and not the "soul" of God? Genesis 2:7 suggests the answer:

"The Lord God formed the man (אָדָם, *adam*, man) of dust (עָפָר, *apher*, dry earth) from the ground (אֲדָמָה, *adamah*, land, from the same word origin as *adam*, man) and breathed (נָפַח, *naphach*, to breathe, to blow) into his nostrils the breath (נְשָׁמָה, *neshamah*, breath, spirit) of life (חַי, *chai*, age), and the man became a living (חַי, *chai*, age) creature (נֶפֶשׁ, *nephesh*, being, creature, self".)

The Holy Spirit is that which endows creatures with life – literally, it inspires (in-spirits) them.

Paul said, "In him we live and move and have our being."[52]

Only when God's Spirit breathed life into Adam's God-created body did Adam become a *nephesh* – a person with a soul.

The Breath or Spirit of God is what animates both the soul and the body. Without the Holy Spirit, neither the soul nor the body can come into existence as a human.

When touched by God's Spirit, a creature becomes alive. When God withholds His Spirit, a creature dies (Psalm 104:29).

The infilling of the Holy Spirit is more than merely being alive – it is a greater awareness and abundance of life as the human temple becomes the dwelling place of God (Romans 8:9-11, 1 Corinthians 12:13, Ephesians 1:13, 1 John 4:13, Isaiah 63:11, John 14:17, Numbers 27:18, Acts 15:8).

By contrast, if a human rejects God's grace, God's Spirit may still keep him alive for the appointed duration of his life, but he may be indwelt by evil spirits, rather than by God's Holy Spirit

(Matthew 12:45). Such a person is alive, but not abundantly alive. Jesus said, "I came that they may have life and have it abundantly." (John 10:10)

The Soul's Path

God created humans as a body-soul unity. Salvation – separation from sin – required an unnatural, but temporary, separation of the body and soul at the moment of physical death.

The saved soul continues immortal, to be re-unified to an immortal body at the final resurrection.

Unsaved souls go to the Lake of Fire.

Saved souls, in rejuvenated immortal bodies, go to Eden restored – the New Heaven and the New Earth.

Our Births and Deaths

God creates everyone, at birth, as a body-soul unity. This is our normal state. Everyone experiences this First Birth.

The First Resurrection is that through Jesus Christ. Only believers have a part in the First Resurrection, because only they are born a second time in Christ. When that happens, they enter Eternal Life – not as a promised future state, but now. Although still in a mortal body, the saved soul, full of the Holy Spirit, is moving toward the doorway of physical death that opens to an eternal state where death no longer occurs.

The First Death, physical death, is the unnatural separation of the body and the soul. Believers and non-believers all experience the First Death. After the First Death, in the intermediate Heaven, the souls of believers are at home with the Lord. After the First Death, in Hades, the intermediate Hell, the souls of unbelievers live in conscious torment apart from God and the saved.

At the Final Judgment, all the dead are raised. For believers, God restores the normal body-soul unity so that they may live in spiritual and physical perfection eternally in the New Earth – which is the final Heaven. Nonbelievers go to age-enduring, conscious torment, apart from God, fellowship, and all joy. Only they experience the Second Death. Believers have no part in that.

Event	Believers	Nonbelievers
First Birth	X	X
Second Birth	X	
First Death	X	X
Second Death		X

How Does Death Happen?

Sinless man was immortal. God mercifully made *fallen* man mortal.

From the standpoint of biology, immortality seems more likely than mortality. It is difficult to explain scientifically why aging and death should occur. Cells regenerate themselves perfectly well for a time – but what gives them a shelf life? Why do organisms reach peak performance and then decline? It is a great mystery of science. There is no inherent reason why created beings should not live forever. So, what originally caused death to become part of life? Put another way, what was the birth of death?

Newton observed a phenomenon called entropy. We cannot explain why entropy should exist, but we can measure it. It is the gradual systematic decay of the universe and the organisms in it. Everything in the universe tends to move from order to disorder, from high energy to low energy, from life to death. Apparently, the mechanism by which God conferred the mercy of physical death on humanity was to introduce entropy into the world.

Scientifically, we have no way to measure whether all the laws of physics came into existence at the time that the universe came into existence.[53] It's probable that most of Newton's Laws of originated simultaneously with the creation of the universe, because these Laws are inherent to the idea of God as Prime Mover and the regulation of matter and energy as they rapidly expanded in the Big Bang.

But what of Newton's Second Law of Thermodynamics? This Law explains that the entropy of a system always increases and is often called the law of increased entropy. Entropy (S) is disorder or chaos in a system.[54] There is no reason why entropy should be inherent to the universe at the time of its creation. Why should it be created to die? Of course, it might have been. But it might also have been created to live forever, and the condition that made it begin slowly and regularly to die might have entered into its essence sometime after its creation.

By introducing entropy – mortality – into the world, God provided that Adam and Eve and their descendants would age and be saved from the unspeakable doom of immortal mortality – endless death.

The poetic words of the Bible – that God "cursed the ground" – describe this concept admirably.

THE INTERMEDIATE HEAVEN

The Bible is perfectly clear about our future after death. 1 Thessalonians 4:13-18 says:

"But we do not want you to be uninformed, brethren, about those who are asleep, so that you will not grieve as do the rest who have no hope.

"For if we believe that Jesus died and rose again, even so God will bring with Him those who have fallen asleep in Jesus.

"For this we say to you by the word of the Lord, that we who are alive and remain until the coming of the Lord, will not precede those who have fallen asleep.

"For the Lord Himself will descend from heaven with a shout, with the voice of the archangel and with the trumpet of God, and the dead in Christ will rise first.

"Then we who are alive and remain will be caught up together with them in the clouds to meet the Lord in the air, and so we shall always be with the Lord. Therefore comfort one another with these words."

When Eden was lost, man's dwelling place became the Earth as we know it. When we die, we go to the Intermediate Heaven or the Intermediate Hell. At Jesus' return, we go to the New Heaven, which is Eden restored or to the permanent Hell, which is Eden forever denied.

Is Intermediate Heaven Eternal?
On Earth, we yearn for the Intermediate Heaven. Paul desired to depart and be with Christ, which is very much better.[55]

But the Intermediate Heaven is temporary. God is everlasting, but the Intermediate Heaven is not. God created Heaven. All created things come into being and change.[56]

Heaven has

- a past (Abraham's bosom for Old Testament saints),
- a present (the Intermediate Heaven for Christians today), and
- a future (the New Heaven and the New Earth).

Hell also changes. God created it, too, and it has

- a past (Sheol for the Old Testament lost),
- a present (Hades for the lost of today), and
- a future – to be thrown, with all its inhabitants and all other unbelievers, into the Lake of Fire.[57]

We inhabit the Intermediate Heaven prior to receiving our final Resurrection Body in the New Earth. In the Intermediate Heaven we await Christ's return to Earth. But there we await that event *together* with Christ.

The Future Heaven

The Future Heaven is the New Earth, in which God and His people will live together in a resurrected universe.[58]

The throne of God and of the Lamb is in the New Jerusalem. Heaven is where God dwells with His people and has His throne – which indicates that the New Jerusalem is there now. [59] Revelation 21 tells us that the New Jerusalem descends from Heaven to the New Earth.[60]

Before the Fall, Eden was a Heaven-Earth unity. Under the curse, the Earth and Heaven are separate.

That God should dwell in unity with us in the end, bringing Heaven and the New Earth together, is consistent with His original and eternal plan – the restoration of Eden.

In Eden, God did not take Adam and Eve to Heaven to commune with them. Instead, God came to walk with them in the Garden.[61]

In the Incarnation, God chose to inhabit time and space as a human being and interact with humanity on this Earth.

In the New Earth, God will make time and space His eternal home with us.

Jesus is God incarnate. The New Earth is Heaven incarnate.

Are We Aware in the Intermediate Heaven (or Hell)?

As the Fall created an unnatural separation between Heaven and Earth, death creates an unnatural separation between our body and spirit, but consciousness does not end for the spirit, even if it does end for the body.

In the parable of the Rich Man and Lazarus,[62] both deceased souls are fully conscious.

Jesus told the thief on the cross that he would be together with Jesus that day in paradise.[63] The promise wouldn't be worth much if the thief were unconscious of its fulfillment.

The Bible tells us that when we die, we are with Christ.[64] Having an unconscious relationship is pointless.

In Revelation, the martyrs in Heaven cry to God for justice on Earth.[65] To do so, they must be aware.

Soul Sleep

Some say that after death we experience "soul sleep." The best Biblical verse to support this is Ecclesiastes 9:5:

"For the living know they will die; but the dead do not know anything, nor have they any longer a reward, for their memory is forgotten. Indeed their love, their hate and their zeal have already perished, and they will no longer have a share in all that is done under the sun."

The better interpretation of this verse is that it describes how death ends a person's ability to participate in life on this Earth – "they will no longer have a share in all that is done under the sun." In other words, it describes the body's sleep, not the soul's.

Other verses in Scripture state clearly that at death the body sleeps, but the soul abides. Daniel 12:2-3 is one example:

"Now at that time Michael, the great prince who stands guard over the sons of your people, will arise. And there will be a time of distress such as never occurred since there was a nation until that time; and at that time your people, everyone who is found written in the book, will be rescued. *Many of those who sleep in the dust of the ground will awake, these to everlasting life, but the others to disgrace and everlasting contempt.*"

2 Corinthians 5:8 is another:

"...we are of good courage, I say, and prefer rather to *be absent from the body and to be at home with the Lord.*"

Judgment after Death

At death, all people face judgment.[66] This is the *first* judgment, which determines who enters the

43

Intermediate Heaven and who enters Hades. This is the judgment of faith. Those who die having faith in Christ go to be with Christ. Those who die unsaved, enter Hades.

The final judgment is a judgment of works, as 2 Corinthians 5:10 says:

"For we must all appear before the judgment seat of Christ, so that each one may be recompensed for his deeds in the body, according to what he has done, whether good or bad."

All means all, saved and unsaved. We *all* give an account of what we did with our incarnate life.

But this judgment does not undermine a believer's salvation. Salvation is a free and absolute gift, as Ephesians 2:8, 9 makes clear, as does Titus 3:5,6:

"He saved us, not on the basis of deeds which we have done in righteousness, but according to His mercy, by the washing of regeneration and renewing by the Holy Spirit, whom He poured out upon us richly through Jesus Christ our Savior."

But the final judgment does affect a believer's *rewards*. Salvation is assured and absolute for those who accept grace. Rewards are conditional, depending on the quality of our faithful works – the fruit of our faith. 2 Timothy 2:12,13 makes this clear:

"It is a trustworthy statement: For if we died with Him, we will also live with Him; If we endure, we will also reign with Him; If we deny Him, He also will deny us; If we are faithless, He remains faithful, for He cannot deny Himself."

Revelation 2:26 Jesus says that to those of us who overcome and keep Christ's deeds until the end, He will give authority over the nations and the right to sit with Jesus on His throne.[67]

Is the Intermediate Heaven Physical?

Heaven normally is invisible. It appears to exist in a dimension inaccessible to us. However, on some occasions, Heaven has become visible.

Stephen saw the heavens open and Jesus sitting on the right hand of God.[68]

Elisha asked God to let his servant Gehazi see the invisible realm, and God opened Gehazi's eyes to a mountain filled with horses and chariots of fire.[69]

Angels are spirit beings and live in Heaven, yet God sometimes empowers them to enter this earthly realm. Hebrews 13:2 says that some have entertained angels without knowing it.

The Bible makes numerous references to physical things in Heaven.

- 2 Kings 2:11 and Revelation 19:14 describe horses in Heaven.
- Revelation 7:9 describes scrolls, elders, martyrs in clothing, and people holding palm branches in the Intermediate Heaven.
- Revelation 8:13 describes a flying eagle in heaven.
- Revelation 8:6 describes musical instruments – and music requires physical sound waves.
- Revelation 15:8 describes a heavenly temple filled with smoke.

Some of these things may be symbols – but would all of them be symbols? A literal interpretation of Scripture would argue against all being symbolic unless Scripture pronounced them all symbolic.

Hebrews 8:5 says that Earth is Heaven's shadow. Since the shadow is merely an effect of something more real than itself, it stands to reason that Heaven is somehow more real, more vital, than Earth. Since Earth has physical attributes, perhaps Heaven has them too – and possibly in more ample dimensions.

The Tree of Life was once physically in Eden. Revelation 2:7 says that now it is now physically in Heaven. Revelation 22:2 says that it will be in the Future Heaven.

After the Fall, God took away man's access to Eden.[70] Cherubim guarded the gateway to Eden. Cherubim are the beings who stand on either side of God's throne, according to 2 Kings 19:15.

The Bible never says that God destroyed Eden. It says the curse destroyed man's access to Eden. God apparently translated Eden into another dimension, because the things that were in Eden – the Tree of Life and Cherubim (and even Adam and Eve) are in the Intermediate Heaven now.

Eden was Heaven's past. The Intermediate Heaven is Eden's present. The New Earth is Eden's future.

Revelation 22:2 depicts the Trees of Life bearing fruit on either side of the river flowing out of the New Jerusalem. This park (paradise) near the City of God sounds very much like Eden restored.

Another Dimension

Since the Intermediate Heaven exists today, where does it exist?

The following is partly extra-Biblical speculation, but it is possible that the question "where" is not precisely relevant to Heaven, in the same way that "How High?" is not a relevant question to a line in the sand.

We exist in four dimensions: length, width, height, and time.

Heaven may exist in a reality which involves a fifth dimension. If so, the location of Heaven might be the same location as Earth – but since the two realities exist in the framework of different dimensions, they do not physically interfere with each other. This is the philosophical concept of "parallel universes."

The Bible possibly supports this idea, since an angel appeared to Balaam's donkey but not to Balaam,[71] the deceased Samuel appeared to Saul,[72] Elijah and Moses appeared with Jesus on the Mount of Transfiguration,[73] the resurrected Jesus moved through locked doors,[74] the Apostle Philip was mystically transported by the Holy Spirit after witnessing to the Ethiopian eunuch,[75] Peter was mystically led out of jail cells by angels,[76] and the Apostles Paul[77] and John[78] were mystically transported to Heaven.

The problem with this and other quantum physical concepts is that while our minds may *apprehend* (grasp) such ideas, we can never fully *comprehend* (wrap our minds around) them. The reason for this is that our minds are bound in four dimensions. We do have the ability to imagine some aspects of life outside of four dimensions, and these logical concepts never impact us fully because we cannot experience their reality.

We can understand this better if we relate ourselves to existence in a world of fewer dimensions than ours. We can both apprehend and comprehend life in a "lower" state; but we can only apprehend but not comprehend life in a "higher" state.

For example, the word on a page in a book exists in two dimensions – width and length. (For the sake of argument, let's assume that the word has no height – that the ink and the surface of the page are flush.)

If we were a word on a page, we might look to words on either side of us, or the words above and below us, but we could not see the top of the page, the bottom of the page, or the edges of the page. We certainly could not see the previous page, the next page, or the beginning or the end or the covers of the book.

But if we were a human being reading the book, existing in three dimensions, we could, at one glance, at one time, see the entire page, top, bottom, edges, as well as the facing page.

Because human beings also exist in time, we could turn the page, and even view the beginning or the end of the book. We could, like God, "know the end from the beginning."[79]

The word on the page might just barely apprehend that this is possible; but it could never comprehend – imagine and experience – the reality of it.

In the same way, we are a word on the page of time. We cannot turn to the first or last pages of time. We cannot even turn to the next chapter. We can remember the last chapter, but only imperfectly. We cannot imagine and experience previous chapters.

And we certainly cannot imagine and experience what it might be like to live with a fifth dimension, one which might permit us to step in and out of time and space just like a person walking through a door – or to process immense tracts of time in an instant.

Modern philosophy and science do admit of such possibilities. For example, we know from physical experimentation that one electron – the same electron – can exist in two places at the same time.

If you shoot an electron through two very closely spaced holes in a metal foil, the electron will actually pass through both holes at the same time! This is the property of ubiquity – being everywhere at once. We call God omnipresent, and skeptics argue that this is impossible, but electrons are created beings, and if created beings require a Creator, and if the Creator must be greater than what is created, then God must possess the property of ubiquity if He is to impart that property to something He creates.

Consider the concept of Jesus' atonement for the sins of the world on the Cross. If many billions of people had sinned, were sinning, or would sin from Creation to the end of time, Jesus would need to atone for all those sins in the space of six hours' torment. A merely human mind could not comprehend – imagine and experience – even the names of so many billions of people, let alone process the detailed courses of their lives, all their daily sins, and pay the price, personally and intimately, for every single one. Impossible. But in theology, it is always necessary to remember that with man many things are impossible, but with God all things are possible. Sherlock Holmes said, "Eliminate the impossible; whatever is left, however improbable must be the truth." In matters of God, we can eliminate things that God has created to be impossible – like "square circles" and "holy sin" – but there is an immensity of improbable things that we cannot eliminate: things impossible for us, but not for Him.

It is philosophically possible that Jesus simply "bleeped" over all the details of all the lives He was atoning for and struggled with the "big picture."

But it is also philosophically possible that the careful embrace of all these details, a process that might take a human mind billions of years and a computer millions of years, was effortlessly possible for the Divine Mind. Why? Because, like a human being turning the pages of a book, God has "all the time" to deal with all of time. Since to God, all times are soon – or even now – He can deal with a million years in a minute. The Bible explicitly states that to God, a thousand years are as a day and a day are as a thousand years.[80]

Physical science, again, supports this concept via Einstein's Theory of Relativity. A moving clock ticks more slowly than a stationary clock. A clock at a higher altitude (farther from gravitational pull) ticks faster than a clock closer to earth.

So, if you are traveling on a star speeding at a million miles per second at the edge of the universe, years on that star may transpire within twenty-four hours on earth.

The Six Days of Creation need not be *either* twenty-four-hour days or million-year days – they can be both. It depends upon the viewpoint of the stopwatch. And if God is holding the stopwatch, His viewpoint transcends time.

Therefore, the Intermediate Heaven can exist "Here and Now," as well as "There and Then" – at a time and place that are superimposed, but not identical, conflicting, or intermixed.

Humanity and Time

When God animated the dust and created Adam, Adam became not merely a *nephesh* – a person – but a "living" person. This word "living" in Hebrew means an *ageing* person. That is, God created humans to dwell in the stream of time just as he

50

created fish to live in water. If one fish asks another, "How is the water?" the second will reply, "What water?" Water is essential to living as a fish, just as time is essential to living as a human.

Prior to the entry of death into the world, ageing did not produce decay. In Heaven, there will be time and we will age – but we will not decay.

Time is the measurement of change. Ageing in Heaven will be a measure of how we change – growing eternally in knowledge, skills, and understanding of our infinite Creator. But the difference between ageing in Heaven and ageing on this fallen earth is that in Heaven, there will be no deterioration. We will grow, but not decline. And there will be no shortage of time; we will never run out of it.

Do We Have Bodies in the Intermediate Heaven?

John 4:24 and Hebrews 1:14 tell us that God and angels are spirits.

Genesis 2:7 shows that human beings, in nature and essence, are both body and spirit.

God created Adam's body first and then breathed spirit into it. Humans never existed until God made Adam as a body-soul unity.

While it is debatable if we have bodies in the Intermediate Heaven, Bible passages make it seem possible – even probable – that we do.

Genesis 5:24 says God took Enoch to Heaven; Hebrews 11:5 states that Enoch did not die. If so, Enoch would appear to be embodied in Heaven.

Elijah in his body was caught up to Heaven in a whirlwind.81 Elijah would appear to be embodied in Heaven.

Moses and Elijah met Christ in their bodies on the Mount of Transfiguration.[82]

In Revelation 6:9-11, the martyrs wear clothes. Wearing clothes requires bodies.

In Revelation 10:9-10, the Apostle John visited Heaven and grasped, held, ate, tasted and measured things there.

When Paul describes visiting Heaven, he relates in 2 Corinthians 12:3 that he wasn't sure if he had a body there – but he wasn't sure that he didn't.

Acts 1:11 tells us that Christ's physical body is in Heaven – and the same Jesus the Apostles saw ascending will return. In Acts 7:56, Stephen sees Jesus standing by God's throne. Jesus seems to be embodied in Heaven.

Are We Conscious in the Intermediate Heaven?
In both the Intermediate Heaven and Hell, Jesus says an hour is coming in which all who are in tombs will hear His voice and come forth, those who did good deeds to a resurrection of life, and those who did evil deeds to a resurrection of judgment.[83]

If those whose earthly bodies are in tombs can hear His voice, to do so they must be conscious somewhere – clearly in the Intermediate Heaven and Hell.

Jesus tells us that there is much rejoicing in Heaven in the presence of angels at one lost soul who is saved.[84] The rejoicing is in the presence of the angels, implying that the saints are rejoicing. To rejoice, they must be conscious.

In Luke 16:19-31, the story of the Rich Man and Lazarus describes
- fire,
- thirst,

- a finger, and
- a tongue.

Some say this parable is allegorical, but it is the only parable in which Jesus specifically names one of the characters, Lazarus. Possibly He was referring to the future, final death of Lazarus, His close friend (whom He raised from the dead once), but in any case, the specific name implies that the parable refers to a real person, not a fictional one.

This story highlights several aspects of the Intermediate Heaven:

- Angels carry Lazarus to Heaven.
- The Rich Man goes to a place of torment.
- Lazarus is with Abraham – he is not alone, and presumably other saints are there, too.
- The Rich Man is alone.
- A fixed and unbridgeable chasm separates the Intermediate Heaven and Hell.
- People on both sides of the chasm can communicate.
- The people in both places maintain their earthly identities.
- They both have physical forms.
- The Rich Man has conscious memory of his lost brothers.

All of this implies that life in the Intermediate Heaven – and Hell – is physical and conscious.

What Do We Know in the Intermediate Heaven?
Revelation 6:9-11 gives us some important indications of life in the Intermediate Heaven:

"When the Lamb broke the fifth seal, I saw underneath the altar the souls of those who had been slain because of the word of God, and because of the testimony which they had maintained; and they cried out with a loud voice, saying,

'How long, O Lord, holy and true, will You refrain from judging and avenging our blood on those who dwell on the earth?'

"And there was given to each of them a white robe; and they were told that they should rest for a little while longer, until the number of their fellow servants and their brethren who were to be killed even as they had been, would be completed also."

The martyrs had the same identity in Heaven as they had on Earth.

They cried out: they were capable of audible expression, which requires physical being (moving air waves).

They were aware of the situation on Earth.

They asked God to intervene – they were in fellowship with God.

They wanted to know the future – they lived in time; they were not all-knowing.

They desired justice and retribution – they lived in time; they look forward to future events.

They remembered their lives on Earth – they knew they had been murdered – they lived in time; they look back on the past.

They each wore a white robe, meaning they must have had bodies for the robes to adorn.

They were connected to the saints on Earth – their fellow servants and brothers.

The story of the Rich Man and Lazarus tells us that those who endured bad things on Earth remember and are comforted in Heaven.

After death, we give an account of our lives. 2 Corinthians 5:10 says:

"For we must all appear before the judgment seat of Christ, so that each one may be recompensed for his deeds in the body, according to what he has done, whether good or bad."

Jesus said:

"But I tell you that every careless word that people speak, they shall give an accounting for it in the day of judgment. For by your words you will be justified, and by your words you will be condemned."[85]

Giving an account of our lives implies perfect memory and clear thought. We will not plead our case deceptively to God. Romans 1:20 says that all who deny God, in spite of the clear evidence of His eternal power and divine nature, are without excuse. Therefore, we will state our cases in perfect justice, uncomfortable as that will be, and with impeccable logic – and perfect, conscious memory.

Therefore, we are conscious in the Intermediate Heaven, have perfect and complete recall of the past, see the present clearly, but do not know the future.

Are People in the Intermediate Heaven Aware of Events on Earth?

Revelation 6:9-11 (above) suggests that they are. In Revelation 18:20, we read that the saints rejoice at the fall of Babylon. In Revelation 19:1-5 the saints give out a roar of praise for the judgment events on Earth.

When God permitted Samuel to return from death and appear to Saul and the witch of Endor,[86] Samuel knew what had happened before his death and was aware of the current events in King Saul's life.

Moses and Elijah spoke with Jesus in the Transfiguration about Jesus' departure, which He was about to accomplish in Jerusalem.[87] They knew

55

the current events on Earth. Isn't it also likely that the two of them discussed their meeting with Jesus upon their return to Heaven?

Hebrews 12:1 says we are surrounded by a great cloud of witnesses – presumably the saints in Heaven. 1 Timothy 3:15 and 5:21 tell us that angels see the events on Earth. 1 Corinthians 4:9 says:

"For, I think, God has exhibited us Apostles last of all, as men condemned to death; because we have become a spectacle to the world, both to angels and to men."

If angels can see events on Earth, why not the departed saints? It seems, therefore, that we can see and follow events on Earth in the Intermediate Heaven.

Do We Pray in the Intermediate Heaven for Those on Earth?

Jesus, who is forever God and Man, intercedes for us in Heaven.[88] In Revelation 6:10, the martyrs in Heaven pray for justice on Earth. If, as James 5:16 tells us, the prayers of a righteous person avail much, our prayers in Heaven would be extremely effective, since our righteousness in Heaven will be complete. Very possibly we do pray in Heaven, and if so, for whom could we better pray than those on Earth?

Can Awareness of Evil on Earth Spoil Heaven's Joy?

Lazarus and Abraham saw the Rich Man in Hell, but Heaven was still Heaven for them. If Jesus in Heaven grieved for Paul's persecution of the church,[89] why should the saints in Heaven not do the same? Yet Paul did not spoil Jesus' perfect peace – the yet unsaved Paul was, in fact, spoiling his own life.

Revelation 21:4 says that God will wipe away our tears and abolish pain and sorrow, but this refers to the Future Heaven, not the Intermediate Heaven in the present. (It also does not say there will be no tears, merely that God will wipe them away.)

It may well be that in the Intermediate Heaven we see the evil on Earth and grieve for it, but the joy of being at home with Christ nevertheless dominates every feeling and thought. Heaven could hardly be Heaven if the evil of mankind could veto God's plan for our happiness.

Grieving on Earth for our Beloved Dead

While sadness at parting is natural and healthy, we should not grieve overly for our departed Christian loved ones. Our separation from them is an interruption, not a loss. 1 Thessalonians 4:13-18 says:

"But we do not want you to be uninformed, brethren, about those who are asleep, so that you will not grieve as do the rest who have no hope.

"For if we believe that Jesus died and rose again, even so God will bring with Him those who have fallen asleep in Jesus.

"For this we say to you by the word of the Lord, that we who are alive and remain until the coming of the Lord, will not precede those who have fallen asleep.

"For the Lord Himself will descend from heaven with a shout, with the voice of the archangel and with the trumpet of God, and the dead in Christ will rise first.

"Then we who are alive and remain will be caught up together with them in the clouds to meet the Lord in the air, and so we shall always be with the Lord. Therefore comfort one another with these words."

THE NEW EARTH

This world, with its natural wonders, is a foretaste of the New Earth. Eating with friends on this Earth is a foretaste of eating with friends on the New Earth. The Great Barrier Reef, the Himalayas, the Tuscan hills, the Amazon basin, Niagara Falls, the African savannah – all foreshadow the New Earth.

Yearning for Eden
Eden is where our hearts long to be.

God's dwelling with man was, is, and will be only in three places:

- Eden
- The Temple (where the high priest officiated), and
- In New Jerusalem.

Types and Shadows
The beauties of our Father's world are reminiscences of Eden long ago, and they are types and shadows of the New Earth to come.

God made Eden for us. He crafted and cultivated Eden. He didn't just let it grow up as a tangle of weeds. Genesis 2:8-9 says:

"The Lord God had *planted* a garden in the east, in Eden; and there He put the man he had formed. And the Lord God *made* all kinds of trees grow out of the ground – trees that were pleasing to the eye and good for food."

God left nothing to chance. He made a perfect home for man and then created man to inhabit it.

Jesus said he went to prepare a place for us.[90] God has prepared the New Earth with the same loving care that He lavished on Eden.

We are in the cursed world, in-between. We live inside a mirror. The perfect world that was and the perfect world to come are the Reality that this dim mirror reflects.

A Better World

But the New Earth is more than a return to Eden. It is an improvement upon Eden.

In Eden, there were no musical instruments. On the New Earth, there will be. In Eden, there was no civilization or technology.

The New Earth will embody the height of civilization and technology. The New Earth will embody the cumulative benefits of human knowledge, art and science.

How do we know? Because the Bible reveals music, architecture, government, civilization, cultivation, and worship in the New Jerusalem. In other words, we will enjoy all the good things that the human race, in God's image, has created over all time.

The music of Mozart, the plays of Shakespeare, the laws of Newton, the inventions of Edison, the speeches of Lincoln, the paintings of Rafael, the sculptures of Praxiteles – all these will be there. The authors of these masterpieces may or may not be in the New Earth – but the fruits of their genius will be.

We have never seen men and women and animals and nature acting and interacting as God intended them to, before the Fall. We have only seen the ruins of their original beauty. Yet we consider the Earth beautiful.

But the Earth is like the backside of a carpet. If the wrong side of Heaven can so inspire us, what must the right side be like?

We will not trade Earth's beauty for Heaven's beauty – Heaven will retain all of Earth's beauty and enhance it. The New Earth will be just as Earthly as the new "us" will be just as identifiably ourselves.

In *The Last Battle,* C.S. Lewis says of the New Earth:

"I have come home at last! This is my real country! I belong here. This is the land I have been looking for all my life, though I never knew it till now. The reason why we loved the old Narnia is that it sometimes looked a little like this...

"'Why!' exclaimed Peter. "It's England. And that's the house itself – Professor Kirk's old home in the country where all our adventures began!'

"'I thought that house had been destroyed,' said Edmund.

"'So it was,' said the Faun. 'But you are now looking at the England within England, the real England just as this is the real Narnia. And in that inner England, no good thing is destroyed.'"

We will not miss this Earth in the New Earth, because in the New Earth, no good thing of this Earth is destroyed.

Our Eternal Purpose

Have you ever felt sad at all the dreams you had that never came true? Or at all the things you wanted to try but never found time to start in this life, let alone to complete and master?

Does it seem probable that God put these dreams in our hearts to tease us? Or is it not more likely that God never intended us to begin, let alone finish, all these dreams in this life? Our purpose here remains our purpose for all time.

The Westminster Shorter Catechism says, "The chief end of man is to glorify God and to enjoy Him for eternity."

Surely we glorify and enjoy God by expressing the talents He has placed in us. The parable of the talents makes this clear. In the parable of the talents, the man who does not multiply his talents is punished. But the men who do multiply their talents are given even greater scope to exercise their talents in eternity.

God means for us to make as much of what we can on this Earth, and to make everything of all we can eternally in the New Earth.

NEW JERUSALEM

Scripture describes Heaven as a country[91] and a city.[92]

Revelation describes architecture, walls, and streets in the New Jerusalem. Cities have citizens, subject to a city government. They have cultural events and business activities.

New Jerusalem is walled, but its gates never close. It is capable of defense, but in the presence of God in a sinless New Earth, its security is absolute.

New Jerusalem is 1,400 miles wide, 1,400 miles high and 1,400 miles long. A city this size would stretch from Canada to Mexico. The area of the city is 1.96 million square miles or more than 1.25 billon acres. New Jerusalem is half the area of the USA.

The Bible doesn't say that all citizens of the New Earth will live in New Jerusalem, but if they did, how many could New Jerusalem hold?

If four families of four people can live on an acre of land (the population density of New York is 15 people per acre), the city would comfortably house 20 billion people.

However, if the city has people living on higher stories and floors (and a city 1,400 miles high probably would), New Jerusalem could have 976,000 stories and could accommodate over 19,000 trillion people.

Is that enough for all saved people? The following chart estimates the number of people who ever have lived on Earth.

How Many People Have Ever Lived on Earth?[93]

Year	Population	Births per 1,000	Births Between Benchmarks
50,000 B.C.	2		
8000 B.C.	5,000,000	80	1,137,789,769
1 A.D.	300,000,000	80	46,025,332,354
1200	450,000,000	60	26,591,343,000
1650	500,000,000	60	12,782,002,453
1750	795,000,000	50	3,171,931,513
1850	1,265,000,000	40	4,046,240,009
1900	1,656,000,000	40	2,900,237,856
1950	2,516,000,000	35	3,390,198,215
1995	5,760,000,000	31	5,427,305,000
2002	6,215,000,000	23	983,987,500
Number who have ever been born			106,456,367,669
World population in mid-2002			6,215,000,000
Percent of those ever born who are living in 2002			5.8

So, perhaps about 100 billion people have ever been born.

Today about one-third of the world's population (6.7 billion in 2008) claims to be Christian. If all of them are saved, and if an equal proportion of all people at all times were saved, that would be 2.2 billion people.

But in the First Century only 0.3% of the world was Christian, and of non-Christians, the percentage of people who were a law unto themselves[94] and therefore saved is hard to guess.

It is evident that all people calling themselves Christians will not be saved. Jesus said that He would reject many who insincerely called Him Lord.[95]

So, if we assume that only 15% of the total number of humans ever born are bound for Heaven, then only 16 billion would inhabit Heaven, while the capacity of New Jerusalem is over 184,000 times that number. The Earth could continue for millennia without this number of people living and dying in a state of grace.

The New Jerusalem is big enough for everyone who will live there.

The World is Improving

The estimated population of the world is a possible indicator of something else. Christians often say the world is getting worse. But, in fact, with the spread of Christianity, it is getting better.

Of course, terrible things still happen. But fewer terrible things happen in terms of events per capita of the Earth's total population.

In the First Century, women and children had the status of slaves. Husbands and fathers could abandon or kill them legally.

In the First Century, there were no hospitals, charities, orphanages or women's shelters. These institutions came into existence as a direct consequence of Jesus' command to care for the sick, for the poor, for orphans, and for widows.

In the First Century, there were just as many wars, rumors of wars, earthquakes and natural disasters as there are today. But in percentage terms, the devastation of these things was far greater.

In 79 A.D., approximately 150,000 people died in Pompeii – 0.05% of the world's population. In the tsunami of 2005, 294,000 people died – 0.005% of the world's population.

About 1.3 million people died in the Jewish-Roman War of A.D. 66-73 – 0.43% of the world's population. About 100 million people died in World Wars I and II combined – 0.05% of the world's population.

In A.D. 100, when the Apostle John died, there were about 1 million Christians in the world – about

0.3% of the world's population. Today, over 2 billion people profess Christianity – about 33% of the world's population.

Thus, the greatest disaster of antiquity claimed ten times more lives, in per capita percentage terms, than the greatest disaster of the 20th century.

The greatest military death toll of the First Century claimed nine times more lives, in per capita percentage terms, than World Wars I and II combined.

There are 110 times more people, in percentage terms, who profess Christ than did so in A.D. 100.

And today even non-Christians frequently acknowledge the morality Christ taught. For example, no person or nation could profess the enslavement and trafficking women and children with impunity today. Of course, people and nations do enslave and traffic women and children, but, to escape the opprobrium of the world, they must pretend that they do not endorse these evils. Before Christ, evil people could do evil deeds without feeling the need to cover their tracks. In fact, sometimes having power to oppress others was a symbol greatness and source of pride.

For example, Herod the Great had no shame at killing all the young boys in Bethlehem. But in the Christian Era, even a man so utterly perverse as Mao Zedong always tried to pretend that his evil acts were just.

Christ set a bright universal standard of morality that evil men might fall beneath, but seldom ignore.

So, the world is in fact getting better as we approach End Times, not worse. And if we are obeying the Great Commission and taking the Gospel to all the nations, isn't that what we should expect?

New Earth Physics

If New Jerusalem is a solid cubic structure, like a mountain, then physical laws might be different on the New Earth, because the force of gravity would cause a cube of that size to condense into a sphere, like a small planet.

However, the cubic dimensions of the city might not depict a solid mass. The city might have towers, spires, and floors. If so, this would not require a change in the laws of physics, although it would demonstrate amazing technology in architecture.

The City Gates

New Jerusalem will have three gates on each side. Since each side is 1,400 miles long, the gates will be about 400 miles apart. They may be a mile high or higher, disappearing and re-appearing in passing clouds. They may be a mile or miles wide – wonders of architectural engineering.

The gates will never be shut.[96] Since all the kingdom's enemies will be cast in the Lake of Fire, there will be no need for defense.

The purpose of the gates will be to emphasize the openness of the City of God to all of God's children, and, probably, to glorify God with their enchanting majesty and beauty.

Paul tells us in Philippians 3:20 that "our citizenship is in Heaven." He means that our citizenship is in Heaven now, but our residence is there in the future.

As Israel once wandered in the wilderness before coming to the Promised Land, we wander on this Intermediate Earth until we come into our Promised Land – the New Earth.

The Character of New Jerusalem

Through the eternally open gates, everyone will have equal access to the city's arts, music, and sports.

The city will have no crime, prostitution, beggars, porn shops, sirens, pollution, traffic jams, hospitals, or litter.

It will shine with the glory of God and its brilliance will be like that of a very precious jewel, like a jasper, as clear as crystal.[97]

The river of the water of life, as clear as crystal, will flow from the throne of God and of the Lamb down the middle of the great street of the city.[98]

On each side of the river will stand the Tree of Life, bearing twelve crops of fruit, yielding its fruit every month.[99] Since the tree stands on both sides of the river, the term "tree" must refer to a large grove of trees, not a single tree.

Since the river flows from the Throne of God through the entire city, depending on where God's Throne stands, the river and the park will be at least 700 miles long. This is about one-sixth the length of the Nile, the Amazon or the Mississippi and easily could be a mile wide. If the Throne of God is along one of the walls or corners of New Jerusalem, the river will be twice as long in its course through the city.

Since the river flows down the city's main street, the street must actually be a giant promenade on either bank. Imagine the Left Bank in Paris, but thousands of times longer, cleaner, and more enchanting! Imagine the recreational possibilities on this long, crystal-clear, life-giving river, flanked by a multi-million-acre beautiful garden! What fish, birds, and animals might abound for the delight of God and humans?

The Tree of Life

The Tree of Life was in Eden. When Adam and Eve fell into a life of constant sin terminated by death, God removed Eden and the Tree of Life from man. God prevented Adam and Eve from eating of the Tree of Life from His mercy. Since the wages of sin are death, had Adam and Eve eaten from this Tree, death would have become immortal. God wished life to be eternal, not death to be immortal.

When the New Jerusalem descends to the New Earth, the Tree of Life already will be in it.

For this reason, it seems logical that Eden, the Tree of Life and the River of Life are in the Intermediate Heaven now. In Revelation, John sees and measures the heavenly Temple. So, the eternal Temple must be there now, too.

As Revelation 2:7 says, "To him who overcomes, I will give the right to eat from the Tree of Life, which is the paradise of God."

If the Tree of Life is the Paradise of God, and if the Paradise of God is Eden, and if the Tree of Life is in Heaven now, then Eden is in the Intermediate Heaven now, and that, most likely, is where we go when we die to live until Christ's Second Coming.

How can we presume this? Not only from the verses above, but from the probability that God did not destroy Eden after Adam and Eve's fall. He simply destroyed man's access to Eden. God made cherubim, who guard God's throne, to guard the entrance to Eden with swords of flame. Perhaps the swords of flame suggest opening a gateway to another dimension, the dimension of Heaven, where Eden abides until the end, when God makes all things new.

In the New Earth, our physical and spiritual life will be restored at their height and will be

everlasting. Revelation 22:2 says that the leav
the Tree of Life are for the healing of the nation

So, there will be nations in the New Earth, but
they will be healed. They will not live in strife but
in harmony and love. And since their nationalities
will be distinct, undoubtedly the beauties of each
culture and language will thrive in the New Earth.
We will enjoy Cajun dancing, balalaika music, and
Kabuki theater.

The Perfect World
We will not have to leave the city to find natural
beauty or leave the country to find the excitement of
the city. In New Jerusalem, the beauties of nature
and civilization will unite, which is what we might
expect, since this city's architect and builder is God.[100]

Nature on the New Earth
Please read Revelation Chapter 21 and Chapter
22:1-5. This gives the full New Testament picture
of the New Heaven and the New Earth. The
Scriptural view of the New Earth is consistent
throughout the Old and New Testaments.

The New Earth will be a resurrection of the First
Earth, but just as the New Jerusalem is almost
indescribably larger, more beautiful and more
inspiring than the Old Jerusalem, the New Earth
surpasses the First Earth, without losing any of its
majesty.

Will there be Time in Heaven?
Jesus says we will be like the angels in the
resurrection, and angels dwell in time. In Daniel's
vision,[101] an angel says,

"But the prince of the kingdom of Persia was
withstanding me for twenty-one days; then behold,
Michael, one of the chief princes, came to help me,

for I had been left there with the kings of Persia. Now I have come to give you an understanding of what will happen to your people in the latter days, for the vision pertains to the days yet future."

The angel was delayed, which means that the angel was operating in time, and the angel understood both the present and the future. Now and the future cannot exist apart from time.

2 Peter 3:8 says that "With the Lord a day is like a thousand years, and a thousand years are like a day."

This is an often-misused verse. It simply means that for God, who inhabits eternity, all times are "soon." Since time is God's creation, it is subject to God. God is not subject to it.

But we are not and never will be like God. God made us time-bound creatures. Time is our natural element, just as water is the natural element for a fish.

What makes us unhappy about time now is not time itself, but entropy.

Newton's Second Law of Thermodynamics describes entropy, or the tendency of the universe to wind down and become less organized. A simple example is this: if you drop a mirror, you expect it to shatter into many pieces. If you drop the many shattered pieces, you do not expect them to organize themselves into the form of a perfect mirror.

Check your child's bedroom and confirm to yourself that things naturally tend to wind down and become less organized, not to wind up and become neater.

Time bothers us because *we* are winding down. We are ageing. We are running out of time.

Time and money wouldn't ever bother us if we never ran out of either. If that were so, no one would ever try to cheat the clock or rob a bank.

We say time is money, by the way. In Modern Greek, the word *lepta* means both time and money. When Greeks say *Den echo lepta*, it can mean either "I don't have time," or "I don't have money."

This is the promise of the New Creation: not an absence of time, but an eternal abundance of it.

Scripture gives us many examples of time in Heaven.

In Luke 15:7, we see that Heaven's inhabitants rejoice when a sinner repents – they track with those moments in time.

In Revelation 6:10, the martyrs in heaven are told to "wait a little longer" when they ask "how long" before Christ will judge the people on earth and avenge their blood. They could not wonder how long or wait unless they were dwelling in time.

In Ephesians 2:7, Paul refers to Christ seated in Heaven in the "ages to come." If Christ presides in Heaven over ages to come, then Earthly time must track somehow with Heavenly time.

Revelation 7:15 says that God's people serve Him day and night in the temple. If so, there must be day and night in Heaven, which is not surprising if Heaven is a New Earth.

Revelation 22:2 says the Tree of Life will yield fruit every month. If so, there must be months, days, hours, seconds, years, centuries, and millennia.

Isaiah 66:22, 23 says that the New Heavens and the New Earth will endure from one new moon to another and from one Sabbath to another. So there are new moons, months, and, yes, weekends in Heaven.

Revelation 8:1 says "there was silence in heaven for about a half an hour."

Revelation shows things happening in heaven as a sequence of events, one after the other, just as they do in time. For example, in Revelation 4:10, we see the saints falling down at God's throne and casting crowns before Him.

In Revelation 5:9-12, the inhabitants of heaven sing. Music has tempo, rhythm, and duration of notes. Music requires time.

Will there be Celestial Bodies in Heaven?

People often conclude that the New Heaven and New Earth will have no sun or moon based on these verses:

And the city has no need of the sun or of the moon to shine on it, for the glory of God has illumined it, and its lamp is the Lamb.[102]

And there will no longer be any night; and they will not have need of the light of a lamp nor the light of the sun, because the Lord God will illumine them; and they will reign forever and ever.[103]

"No longer will you have the sun for light by day, nor for brightness will the moon give you light; but you will have the Lord for an everlasting light, and your God for your glory. Your sun will no longer set, nor will your moon wane; for you will have the Lord for an everlasting light, and the days of your mourning will be over."[104]

The verses do not actually say that there will be no sun or moon, but that the New Earth will not *need* the sun and the moon to provide light, because God will be the source of light.

Since Revelation 7 says there will be day and night, and Revelation 21 says there will be no night, we have these choices:

1. Scripture contradicts itself. Since the evidence for Scripture's inerrancy is compelling, this is the less logical choice.
2. One of the references to night is metaphorical.

If Revelation 7 is metaphorical, then by saying that God's people worship him day and night in Heaven, John is simply saying that they worship God continually.

If Revelation 21 is metaphorical, it means that there will no longer be any night in the sense that there will be no time in which we cannot see, experience fear or danger, or lapse into involuntary inactivity. In this case, the absence of night does not mean that there will not be a night sky, but that God's light will illuminate Heaven and Earth, no matter what the time of day. The beauties of night will still exist in the New Earth. We might even be able to see in the dark.

Since the New Earth is God's New Creation, complete and entire, this seems a preferable interpretation. But can there be an Earth in which the existence of day and night are not inextricably tied to the sun? Yes. And we can cross-check this assertion with Scripture.

In Genesis, God created light and time and day and night on the First Day, before He created the sun and the moon.

"Then God said, "Let there be light"; and there was light. God saw that the light was good; and God separated the light from the darkness. God called the light day, and the darkness He called night. And there was evening and there was morning, one day."[105]

On the Fourth Day, God created celestial bodies and appointed them to impart light to the Earth.

Whose light? Their own? No, the light God imparted to them.

"God made the two great lights, the greater light to govern the day, and the lesser light to govern the night; He made the stars also. God placed them in the expanse of the heavens to give light on the earth, and to govern the day and the night, and to separate the light from the darkness; and God saw that it was good. There was evening and there was morning, a fourth day."[106]

This is further indication that the New Heaven and New Earth are a resurrection of the original Creation.

Will there be Weather in Heaven?
Job 37:3-6 says that lightening, thunder, rain and snow declare God's greatness. Jeremiah 5:24 says that God "gives autumn and spring rains in season." Hebrews 6:7 says that rain is God's blessing on the earth. Psalm 104 describes how lovingly God provides for His creation through Nature.

It is hard to believe, if God will make all things new, that He would make a New Heaven and New Earth without the beauties of weather.

We know certainly from Scripture that there will be months and Sabbaths in Heaven. If there are seasons, and since the hallmark of seasons is weather, probably there will be weather in Heaven.

But there will not be harmful or destructive weather, since that causes of grief and injury, and the Bible assures us that neither of these will exist in the New Heaven and the New Earth.

Will the New Earth Have Any Sea?
If you love the beach, it's rather sad to think that there will no longer be any sea. But Revelation 21:1 says, "Then I saw a new heaven and a new earth;

for the first heaven and the first earth passed away, and there is no longer *any* sea."

However, Revelation 21 doesn't exactly say there will be no new sea or ocean on the New Earth. Verse one says the following:

1. John saw a new heaven and a new earth, for
2. The first heaven and the first earth passed away, and
3. There is no longer any sea.

For there no longer to be any sea, the existing sea would have to pass away. Since the first earth passes away, and since the existing sea is part of the first earth, the sea must pass away with the first earth.

John may be referring to the passing away of the first earth, including the sea, and the first heaven.

The replacement of the first earth with a new earth strongly suggests the recreation of the sea, for several reasons:

In Revelation 21:5 God says He is making all things new. All means all, and that's all that all means. The sea is included in what God originally created, and to create all things new, God would need and want to recreate the sea, as well.

In all other aspects of the New Creation, we see that God compromises none of the beauty of His original Creation. He even improves upon it.

If God does not re-create the sea, He would either have to discard all the sea creatures or they would have to live in another large body of water. We have already seen that the River of Life is at least 700 miles long and may be as much as one mile wide. However, those are its minimum dimensions from its source to the edge of New Jerusalem. Unless the River goes underground at the city's edge, it may continue to flow through the countryside and empty, eventually, into a larger body of water…namely, the sea.

To discard the sea, which was part of the First Creation, would imply that God would have made a more perfect world, one without a sea, if He had had the chance.

But, philosophically, there is no such thing as chance. There is only cause and effect.

Consider a coin toss. You call the result chance only because you don't know all the facts. If you knew in advance the force with which the coin would be flipped, the number of times it would turn, the air resistance, the weight and condition of the coin, the distance the coin would travel, the resistance offered by the surface on which the coin would land, and so on, you could predict heads or tails 100% of the time.

Just as a conclusion is what most people arrive at when they get tired of thinking, chance is what people call cause and effect when they simply don't have the facts or are too lazy to get them.

C.S. Lewis aptly wrote that there are two sides to every question, until you know the answer, and then there is only one.

Since God is in possession of all the facts, is not too lazy to gather them, is intellectually powerful enough to compute them without error, and has no constraints of time, space, or matter, it really is illogical to believe that God's First Creation was a failed attempt.

God created the world exactly as He wanted it, including mankind's free choice, which allowed the possibility of evil, not the necessity of it. The fact that we all choose to do evil every day is our problem not God's.

The fact that God gave us this possibility is a measure of His generosity.

If you did not have a million dollars, you would not have the problem of wondering how to spend it morally; you would not have that choice.

If you did not have free will, you would not have to struggle to choose the right thing; you would have no choice.

Yet, which of us would reject a million dollars if offered to us with only one string attached: that we could spend it any way we like?

Which of us would accept a world in which God took from us our ability to make our own choices?

Since clearly we would hate that, we have to accept the consequences of our own decisions. We do make bad choices every day, and those bad choices entangle us in the terrible net of sin.

From before the foundation of the world, God understood this, created the First Heaven and the First Earth understanding it, included the gift of free will in His Creation, and included a plan for mankind's salvation prior not only to the first sin, but prior to the creation of any being, whether angel or man, to commit that first sin.

Since God's First Creation was perfect, even though it contained the freedom in it for us to spoil its perfection, God's premeditated resurrection of Creation is perfect, including all He intended Creation to be and to become.

Hence, it seems virtually certain that the New Earth will contain seas and oceans to restore what God created in the original Earth and restored following the great flood.

Will There be Animals in Heaven?
God is not in the business of scrapping His Creation. He is in the business of redeeming and

renewing His Creation. The original, perfect Creation included animals. In fact, God delighted in displaying immense diversity of zoology to Adam and allowed Adam to invent their names.

"Out of the ground the Lord God formed every beast of the field and every bird of the sky and brought them to the man to see what he would call them; and whatever the man called a living creature, that was its name. The man gave names to all the cattle, and to the birds of the sky, and to every beast of the field..."[107]

Since God will make all things new, it is hard to imagine how all things would fail to include animals. Also, since heaven will clearly contain plants and fruits, why would it fail to contain animals?

Verses like this one from Isaiah seem to clinch the point:

"'The wolf and the lamb will graze together, and the lion will eat straw like the ox; and dust will be the serpent's food. They will do no evil or harm in all My holy mountain,' says the Lord."[108]

Will Our Beloved Pets be in Heaven?

Scripture does not provide clear assurance of this. However, there seems no reason why the pets we love would be missing from Heaven. Pets are not responsible for choosing to accept or reject the gift of salvation, so we should not expect animals to be in Hell for rejecting fellowship with God. On the contrary, animals yearn for God's intimacy and provision.

"They [the wild animals] all wait for You to give them their food in due season. You give to them, they gather it up; You open Your hand, they are satisfied with good. You hide Your face, they are dismayed; You take away their spirit, they expire and return to their dust. You send forth Your Spirit, they are created; and You renew the face of the ground."[109]

Animals clearly do have a kind of soul, even if it is not the same kind as ours, made in God's image. The spirit of animals responds to love and affection and expresses loyalty and trust.

If God will make all things new, and if He will give eternal fellowship to saved humans, and if He will endow the New Creation with the full panoply of animals, who also will not suffer death there, why might He not also make our familiar pets new?

While we cannot dogmatically assert that this is true, neither can we dogmatically assert that it is false.

What we can dogmatically assert is that our eternal state will be one of consummate happiness; if having our pets with us eternally is necessary for that fullness of joy, God will provide that they will be there.

The New Earth in the Old and New Testaments

The Bible's vision of Heaven is consistent. Isaiah, John, and Peter show us the same view of our future.

In the New Testament, the most important passages are in 2 Peter and Revelation 21 and 22. Isaiah 66 contains the most important comparative passages in the Old Testament.

Such similarity exists between all these passages, that there can be little doubt that they all refer to the same New Creation.

Since all the passages refer to creating a New Heaven and a New Earth, there can be no doubt that the passages do not refer to:

Israel's return to Jerusalem from the Babylonian Captivity, because God did not create a New Heaven or a New Earth then.

Israel's restoration in 1948, because God did not create a New Heaven or a New Earth then.

A Millennial Reign, because proponents of a Millennial Reign suggest that Christ will reign for one thousand years on *this* Earth, not on a newly created Earth, and that God's creation of a New Heaven and New Earth occurs at Christ's final advent, corresponding to the End of Time and Renewal of all things described in Revelation 21.

Isaiah 65

"'For behold, I create new heavens and a new earth; and the former things will not be remembered or come to mind.

"'But be glad and rejoice forever in what I create; for behold, I create Jerusalem for rejoicing and her people for gladness. I will also rejoice in Jerusalem and be glad in My people; And there will no longer be heard in her the voice of weeping and the sound of crying.

"'No longer will there be in it an infant who lives but a few days, or an old man who does not live out his days; for the youth will die at the age of one hundred and the one who does not reach the age of one hundred will be thought accursed.

"'They will build houses and inhabit them; they will also plant vineyards and eat their fruit. They will not build and another inhabit, they will not plant and another eat; for as the lifetime of a tree, so will be the days of My people, and My chosen ones will wear out the work of their hands.

"'They will not labor in vain, or bear children for calamity; for they are the offspring of those blessed by the Lord, and their descendants with them.

"'It will also come to pass that before they call, I will answer; and while they are still speaking, I will hear.

"'The wolf and the lamb will graze together, and the lion will eat straw like the ox; and dust will be the serpent's food. They will do no evil or harm in all My holy mountain,' says the Lord.'"[110]

Will the Old Earth be Forgotten?

We have already seen so many other Scriptural references to our continuing, personal, intellectual awareness in Heaven that we cannot take Isaiah 65:17 to mean that we will have amnesia about the First Creation or about our lives in it.

Since the interpretation of any literature, including God's word, requires us to take words in context and according to their plain meaning, and since Scripture elsewhere says we will remember details of our lives on Earth, clearly this passage simply means that we will not remember the First Earth in such a way that we will long for it in comparison with the New Earth. In other words, why be nostalgic about the old Eden when you are living in a new and better one?

To What Does Isaiah 65 Refer?

Does this passage refer to a restored Jerusalem after the Babylonian Captivity, in today's Israel, or in a Millennial Reign?

Since the features described in this passage refer to a newly created heaven and earth, none of these options is possible. This Jerusalem is the New Jerusalem of Revelation 21.

How can a Youth Die at One Hundred?

If Isaiah 65 refers to the New Heaven and the New Earth, how can a youth die at the age of one hundred and the one who does not live to the age of one hundred be thought accursed? How can there be infants, youths, or old men?

These statements seem to argue that these verses do refer to some time and place other than the New Earth. Let's examine which they might fit.

This cannot refer to Jerusalem after the Babylonian Captivity, because such conditions did not prevail in Israel from the fifth century B.C. to 70 A.D.

This cannot refer to Israel today, because such conditions do not prevail there now.

There is nothing about a Millennial Reign that would preclude long lives, as in the days before Noah, but the passage also says that these events occur in a New Heaven and New Earth, which the Millennial Reign is not, and that there will no longer be heard in Jerusalem the voice of weeping and the sound of crying.

If, at the end of the Millennium, a vast number of humans will rise up to fight Christ and His people in a final battle, clearly a vast number of humans will not be saved in the Millennium. If they are not saved, and if Jesus rules them with a rod of iron, it is illogical to think that there will be no weeping.

Jesus and the saved might weep at their heading to eternal condemnation.

Jesus and the saved might weep at the evil that the unsaved do and the harm they cause others, if only in the final battle.

The unsaved might weep at the misery that their sins cause themselves and others.

The unsaved might weep when they lose the final battle and land in the Lake of Fire.

How Can Isaiah 65 Refer to Infants and Old Men?

If the conditions in Isaiah 65 are not about a Millennial Reign, how can they refer to a New Heaven and New Earth if they also refer to infants, youths, and old men?

On this Earth, infants sometimes live but a few days. In the New Earth, that will not happen.

On this Earth, an old man sometimes does not live out his days. In the New Earth, that will not happen.

To say that in the New Earth a youth will die at the age of one hundred and that the one who does not reach the age of one hundred will be thought accursed is a poetic metaphor, referring to eternal life, not long life. How can we be sure?

Because if a youth died at the age of one hundred, he either would no longer be a youth, but an old man, or, if his youth endured for one hundred years but then he died, he would be cut off in his youth. In this earth, being cut off in one's youth would be considered a tragic event, a cause for weeping.

If a person living eternally should die at the age of one hundred, that would certainly be accursed; but since this will be a place of blessing and free from the curse of death, this simply will not happen.

The choice of 100 years is symbolic. The patriarchs before Noah lived far more than 100 years. Will God's children in the New Earth live shorter lives than they, who were under the curse of sin?

Conclusion: the meaning of verse 20, taken in context of the rest of the passage, is that the sorrow of death that people bear in this cursed Creation will be lifted in the New Creation.

To cross-check this concept with Scripture, let's look at 1 Corinthians 15:54,55,

"But when this perishable will have put on the imperishable, and this mortal will have put on immortality, then will come about the saying that is written, Death is swallowed up in victory. O death, where is your victory? O death, where is your sting?"

Why Does Isaiah 65 Say Children Will Still Be Born?

If this is the New Heaven and New Earth, why does the passage say we will be bearing children?

Actually, verse 23 does not say we *will* bear children. It says we will *not* bear them *for calamity*. It says our offspring and descendants will be with us and blessed by the Lord.

Notice the verses do say that we will labor, but not in vain, we will build, inhabit, work with our hands, have immediate and refreshing dialog with God personally, and live in harmony with all creatures, with no evil or harm on God's holy mountain.

Isaiah 66

"'For just as the new heavens and the new earth which I make will endure before Me,' declares the Lord, 'So your offspring and your name will endure. And it shall be from new moon to new moon and from Sabbath to Sabbath, all mankind will come to bow down before Me,' says the Lord.

"Then they will go forth and look on the corpses of the men who have transgressed against Me. For their worm will not die and their fire will not be quenched; and they will be abhorrence to all mankind.'"[111]

What Jerusalem Does Isaiah 66 Mean?

Does this refer to a restored Jerusalem after Babylon, now, or in the Millennium?

None of these things happened in Israel after the Babylonian Captivity or are happening in Israel now.

It is possible that these things might happen in a Millennial Reign, but not too likely, because:

If all mankind will bow before God, what about those who rebel against God at the end of the Millennium?

Since those who bow down are the same as those who go and look at the corpses of the men who transgressed against God, they cannot be the people of the Millennium. If they were, only some of the people, not all mankind, would bow down, or the people who bow down would be those who were left after the last great battle, and, consequently, after the close of the Millennium.

The implication in verse 22 is that these obedient offspring of God's people are dwelling in the New Heaven and New Earth, because God says they will endure in the same way that the New Heaven and New Earth endure. If in the same way, it may be reasonable to think that God also means at the same place and time.

By the way, this is another proof that time exists in the New Heaven and the New Earth, since God says that they will endure. To endure means to exist over time.

2 Peter 3

"But the day of the Lord will come like a thief, in which the heavens will pass away with a roar and the elements will be destroyed with intense heat, and the earth and its works will be burned up.

"Since all these things are to be destroyed in this way, what sort of people ought you to be in holy conduct and godliness, looking for and hastening the coming of the day of God, because of which the heavens will be destroyed by burning, and the elements will melt with intense heat!

"But according to His promise we are looking for new heavens and a new earth, in which righteousness dwells."[112]

Observations

Peter's prophecy squares entirely with John's:

At Christ's final return, God will destroy this Heaven and this Earth.

He will create a New Heaven and New Earth, in which righteousness dwells.

We who belong to Jesus have His promise that we may look forward to the New Heaven and the New Earth as our home.

LIFE IN HEAVEN

Our Physical, Eternal State

We should expect to be physical human beings living in a resurrected, physical universe.

Jesus gives a foretaste of this, when he says, "Touch me and see; a ghost does not have flesh and bones, as you see I have."[113]

Paul wrote, "For if we have become united with *Him* in the likeness of His death, certainly we shall also be *in the likeness* of His resurrection..."[114]

Will We Be Ghosts?

No. When Jesus appeared after the Resurrection, He said, "Look at my hands and my feet. It is I myself! Touch me and see; a ghost does not have flesh and bones, as you see I have."[115]

By the way, "ghost" in this verse is the Greek word *pneuma* or "spirit." So, there is no Biblical endorsement of ghosts in this passage.

Will We Retain Our Identities?

Yes, emphatically.

Job said, "In my flesh I will see God...I, and not another."[116]

Jesus called people in Heaven by name, including Lazarus, Abraham, Isaac, and Jacob. He said, "I say to you that many will come from east and west, and recline *at the table* with Abraham, Isaac and Jacob in the kingdom of heaven."[117]

And He said of the Father, "I am the God of Abraham, and the God of Isaac, and the God of Jacob. He is not the God of the dead but of the living."[118]

Heaven rejoices over each individual person who is saved.[119]

When Jesus described the final judgment,[120] He explained how those who gave food, water, shelter, clothing, and comfort to the needy will inherit the kingdom prepared from before the foundation of the world, while those who did not do these things will go away to eternal punishment. If judgment is based on an individual's acceptance of grace and upon the acts that testify to salvation, or the lack of these things, it requires individuality.

God did not create a human race of indistinguishable, nameless masses. Each human has a unique genetic code, fingerprints, and identity. There is no good argument for assuming that the eternal state puts an end to recognizable personality.

The same person who becomes absent from the body at death is the same person who becomes present with the Lord.[121]

The Nature of Angels

Angels are created beings.

Psalm 148 calls on all Creation, including angels, to praise God because "He commanded and they were created."

Job 38:4-7 says that angels were present, shouting for joy, as God created the earth. God created angels before He created the world.

John 1:1-3 and Colossians 1:16 state that by Christ all things were created, which means Jesus created angels.

Angels have distinct identities. They have names, like Michael and Gabriel.

Angels cannot die, as Jesus says in Luke 20:36.

Hebrews 1:14 says they are ministering spirits, and spirits, as Jesus says in Luke 24:39, do not have flesh and bones.

So, angels are individual creatures of spirit, while humans are individual creatures of body and spirit.

Nevertheless, angels sometimes have the power to appear and interact with humans in the physical world; however, that ability never appears in Scripture without God granting or commanding it. Even Satan's ability to afflict Job was only possible when God allowed it.

Will We Become Angels?

We will not become angels. Angels and humans are different types of created beings and will remain distinct in the eternal state.

Death is a relocation of the same person from one place to another. Death is not the transformation of someone from one ontological identity to another. Humans neither become angels nor dogs in Heaven.

In heaven, human beings will govern angels.[122]

The following verse leads some to believe we will become angels.

Matthew 22:30 "For in the resurrection they neither marry nor are given in marriage but are like angels in heaven."

But Jesus does not say that humans in the resurrection will *become* angels, but that we will be *like* angels, and like them in the sense of neither marrying nor being given in marriage.

Strictly speaking, it doesn't even say we won't be married, but that we won't be *getting* married. Although Jesus makes this statement with respect to a woman who had several husbands, it doesn't say she won't have any spouse in heaven, but that there won't be trouble about which one it is.

Perhaps she'll spend time in heaven with the husband who was her closest soul-companion on earth.

Or perhaps she will have a sisterly relationship with all of her spouses that reach heaven – because not all of them might. In fact, none of them might.

All we can absolutely deduce from this is that there won't be polygamy in heaven, that there won't be jealous rivalry in heaven, and that there won't be courtship and weddings in heaven.

Will We Have Special Love Relationships?
We can be sure that we will retain our identities in heaven, be recognizable and memorable to everyone we meet.

If we especially love a spouse (or anyone else) on earth, we will renew the fullness of that special love in heaven, without any of the constraints or flaws of relationships on earth, provided our beloved has also accepted Christ's gift of grace and will therefore be in Heaven.

For example, Jesus seems to have been particularly fond of John, Lazarus, Martha and Mary. There is no reason why they should not renew and enjoy that special love in the eternal state.

But there is also no reason to expect that anyone else should feel jealous of those friendships, because God will grant us fullness of joy in our relationship to Him, to each other, and to all Creation.

As for people who die without ever having been married, we can feel sure, since there will be no unhappiness in heaven, that they will find companionship equally as fulfilling as all those who reunite with beloved spouses in heaven.

Will We Have Emotions?

The Bible describes God as enjoying, loving, laughing, delighting, rejoicing, being angry, happy, jealous, and glad.

Anthropomorphism is attributing human characteristics to something that is not human. With respect to God, however, we have it backwards. Emotions are *godly* attributes mirrored in human beings, not *human* attributes mirrored in God.

We reflect His glory. He does not reflect our glory.

The Bible says, "He will wipe away every tear from their eyes; and there will no longer be any death; there will no longer be any mourning, or crying, or pain."[123]

If God will wipe away tears, there must be tears to wipe away. But the tears will not be those of mourning, crying or pain.

Note that the word "crying" here does not mean weeping, but outcry or shouting. The Greek word is *kraugi*. The same word occurs in these verses:

"But at midnight there was a shout [kraugi], 'Behold, the bridegroom! Come out to meet him.'"[124]

"And there occurred a great uproar [kraugi]; and some of the scribes of the Pharisaic party stood up and began to argue heatedly, saying, 'We find nothing wrong with this man; suppose a spirit or an angel has spoken to him?'"[125]

So, we may shed tears, but we will not cry out, suffer or grieve. We will experience emotions in heaven, without, as on earth, ever needing to be afraid of our feelings.

Why would we shed tears, then? Perhaps, reflecting on the injustices, failures, and losses we suffered on earth, we will remember our grief, and weep that we have been saved from so many things, but we will weep tears of gratitude, in the realization that those wounds are forever healed.

Will We Have Desires?

Yes, but never illicit ones. We will feel attraction without lust, loyalty without betrayal, love without jealousy, appetite without gluttony, and adventure without risk.

Psalm 37:4 says "Delight yourself in the Lord and He will give you the desires of your heart."

The person who *wants* to do what he *must* do is free. If you are a writer, and you *must* write to live, and you *love* writing, you are free.

The person who *hates* to do what he *must* do is a slave. If you are a writer and you *must* write to live and you *hate* writing, you are a slave.

Whoever wants to do what God wants him to do is free. Whoever is saved in Christ has the Spirit within him and is free for this reason. Even if he sins, he feels badly about it. If he does God's will, he feels good about it. He is free to do what God wants him to do, and deep down, that's what he also wants. He acts from love and produces good fruit.

"But the fruit of the Spirit is love, joy, peace, patience, kindness, goodness, faithfulness, gentleness, self-control; against such things there is no law."[126]

Notice that all the fruits of the Spirit proceed from love; if you act from love, you can hardly be otherwise.

Whoever wants to do what God does not want him to do is a slave to the flesh. He acts from selfishness (the opposite of love), produces bad fruit and feels miserable about life.

" Now the deeds of the flesh are evident, which are: immorality, impurity, sensuality, idolatry, sorcery, enmities, strife, jealousy, outbursts of anger, disputes, dissensions, factions, envying, drunkenness, carousing, and things like these, of which I forewarn you, just as I have forewarned you, that those who practice such things will not inherit the kingdom of God."[127]

Notice that all the deeds of the flesh are selfish. You can't do any of these things if you are acting out of love.

On this Earth, the Law restrains the Flesh, but only through our *attempted* obedience, which always fails. When we are saved, the Spirit inspires the Flesh, through love, which never fails.

"Love is patient, love is kind. It does not envy, it does not boast, it is not proud. It is not rude, it is not self-seeking, it is not easily angered, it keeps no record of wrongs. Love does not delight in evil but rejoices with the truth. It always protects, always trusts, always hopes, always perseveres. Love never fails."[128]

On this Earth, freedom in Christ comes because we no longer need fear failing the impossible task of keeping the whole Law in all its details. Freedom comes because our conscience is clear; we do not dread the awful consequences of condemnation, because Christ has taken our condemnation upon Himself.

In Heaven we will have desires, but they will all be good and rewarding. We will be able to do whatever we want, because in a state of intimacy with God and righteousness, whatever we want will be what He wants for us, and whatever He wants for us will be what we want.

No Faith or Hope in Heaven

Faith, hope, and love abide, but the greatest of these is love.[129]

Love is greater than faith or hope, because faith and hope are temporary, made for this world, not the eternal state.

In Heaven, you don't need faith, because faith is the "hope of things hoped for, the conviction of things not seen."[130]

In Heaven there will not be things unseen: "For now we see in a mirror dimly, but then face to face; now I know in part, but then I will know fully, just as I also have been fully known."[131]

In the eternal state, you don't need hope, for, "…in hope we have been saved, but hope that is seen is not hope, for who hopes for what he already sees?"[132]

In Heaven we will be in the condition that already fulfills and more than fulfills all hope.

Will We Sin?

If we have free will in Heaven, does that imply the freedom to choose sin? Adam and Eve lived in sinless Eden, and they chose sin. Why should we in the New Eden be immune?

Romans 6:23 says that the wages of sin is death.

Revelation 21:4 says that there will be no more death or mourning or crying or pain, for the old order of things has passed away.

Hebrews 9:26-28 and 10:10 and 1 Peter 3:18 says that Christ only had to suffer once for our sins forever.

2 Corinthians 5:21 says that Christ, who knew no sin, became sin on our behalf, so we would become the very righteousness of God.

Hebrews 10:14 says that Christ's one offering has perfected once for all time those who have been sanctified.

1 Corinthians 15:52 says that we will be raised incorruptible.

Romans 6:7 says that "anyone who has died has been freed from sin."

So, we will not sin in Heaven because we will be incapable of it. We will be like Christ in that we will desire what God wants, and God cannot want sin, since sin, by definition, is a departure from God's will.

A Sunday school teacher once asked a little boy, "What is a sin of omission?"

The boy replied, "A sin I should have committed, but didn't."

God forbids only things that hurt us. He does not make laws because He needs us to follow them. He needs nothing from anyone. He makes laws because we need to follow them to be happy.

We won't sin in Heaven because we'll know better. Now we see as through a glass darkly, then we will see face to face. Now we don't always get it; then we will.

Being unable to sin doesn't mean that we will be robots. You are unable to be a hamster, but that fact doesn't deprive you of your free will.

Imagine having a million dollars and being free to spend them any way you like. On this fallen Earth, you might choose to

1. Send Bibles to China
2. Invite all your friends on a round-the-world cruise
3. Build a palace
4. Spend the rest of your life in a drunken haze
5. Create a mafia empire of your own

6. Or hire a hit man and take revenge on someone you hate.

If you had the million dollars in the New Earth, but only selected choices 1-3, would you lack free will? If you already knew in advance that selecting choices 4-6 wouldn't really make you happy, would having the wisdom not to want them mean you lacked free will?

We will not sin in Heaven for the same reason that Jesus did not sin on Earth. He simply knew too much to make destructive choices.

Will We Learn in Heaven?

In 1 Corinthians 3:12, Paul says that "Now we see as through a glass darkly; then we shall see face to face. Now I know in part; then I shall know fully, even as I am fully known."

Paul says he will know fully, not that he will know everything. Only God is omniscient.

1 Peter 1:12 describes angels in Heaven longing to look into the truths of God. They don't know everything, but they want to learn.

Ephesians 2:6-7 says that "God raised us up with Christ and seated us with Him in the heavenly realms in Christ Jesus, in order that in the coming ages he might show the incomparable riches of His grace."

This indicates an ongoing revelation of God's riches to us.

In fact, in Revelation 21:5, Jesus says, "I am making all things new." Not "I have made," but "I am making." Ongoing.

2 Corinthians 3:8 says that we are continuously "transformed into his likeness with ever-increasing glory."

Jonathan Edwards wrote that "The saints will be progressive in knowledge to all eternity. The number of ideas of the saints shall increase to eternity."

Martin Luther said, "If God had all the answers in His right hand, and the struggle to reach those answers in His left, I would choose the left hand."

We are happy not by just by knowing the truth, but through the process of attaining it. Not only will we learn from God through eternity, we will learn from each other. And we will join Isaac Newton, Galileo, Aquinas, Augustine, Paul, C.S. Lewis, Lincoln, Victor Hugo, Leo Tolstoy, Michelangelo, Handel, and Bach as they work out new ideas, all to the greater glory of God.

Will We All Have Beautiful Bodies?

One of Christianity's greatest thinkers, Augustine of Hippo, wrote in his book, *The City of God:*

"The body shall be of that size which it either had attained or should have attained in the flower of its youth and shall enjoy the beauty that arises from preserving symmetry and proportion in all its members...overgrown and emaciated persons need not fear that they shall be in heaven of such a figure as they would not be even in this world if they could help it."

We will look the way God created us to look, but we will be at our finest, our fittest, and in our peak time of life.

Will Our Bodies Have New Abilities?

We should expect to have the same five senses we have on earth.

Christ's resurrection body could appear and disappear suddenly, pass through locked doors and defy gravity. Many passages in Scripture say our resurrection body will be like Christ's. However, Jesus is God and we shall never be God.

We may have abilities *like* those Jesus demonstrated, or we may not. We can conjecture, but Scripture does not say for sure.

Will We Eat in Heaven?
Yes. Luke 22:29-30: "...and just as My Father has granted Me a kingdom, I grant you that you may eat and drink at My table in My kingdom, and you will sit on thrones judging the twelve tribes of Israel."

Isaiah 25:6-8: "The Lord of hosts will prepare a lavish banquet for all peoples on this mountain; a banquet of aged wine, choice pieces with marrow, *and* refined, aged wine."

If we don't have intermediate bodies in the intermediate heaven (a point on which we can't be absolutely sure from Scripture), then we won't eat; but if we do have temporary bodies, we might.

Psalm 78:25 refers to manna as the "bread of angels."

The Tree of Life grows in the present Heaven, and God says those who overcome may eat of it.[133]

Perhaps they won't eat of it until New Jerusalem descends to the New Earth, but they might.

In the eternal state, however, the likelihood of eating and drinking is almost beyond debate.

Jesus ate real food with His disciples on the shore of Lake Galilee after His resurrection.[134]

Philippians 3:21 says that Christ will "transform our lowly bodies so that they will be like His glorious body."

In Luke 22:18, Jesus told His disciples, "I tell you I will not drink again of the fruit of the vine until the kingdom of God comes."

In Matthew 8:11, Jesus says, "Many will come from the east and the west and will take their places at the feast with Abraham, Isaac, and Jacob in the kingdom of heaven."

In Revelation 19:9, an angel in Heaven told John, "Blessed are those who are invited to the wedding supper of the Lamb!"

Luke 14:15 says, "Blessed is the man who will eat at the feast of in the kingdom of God."

We will surely eat in Heaven – and I hope that in Heaven celery will be fattening and bread will not!

Will We Be Hungry?

In 1 Corinthians 6:13, Paul says that food is for the stomach and the stomach is for food, but someday God will do away with both of them.

Yes, God will do away with both of them, because our bodies will die and He will destroy the Earth. However, He will also resurrect our bodies and create a New Heaven and a New Earth. He will create all things new, which undoubtedly means what it says, including stomachs and food. Paul is simply saying that we should live in this life with an eye on eternity, not as slaves to our desires.

Revelation 7:16 says that never again will we hunger or thirst. But Revelation 7:17 says that the Lamb will be our shepherd and will lead us to springs of living water. These verses simply say that we our needs will be met, not that we will have no needs.

It is certainly possible that God may resurrect our bodies in such a way that we never feel hunger; but since hunger and satisfying hunger are part of the joy of eating, it seems reasonable that these desires and the satisfaction of them will be part of our eternal state.

How Will Food Taste?

1 Corinthians 10:31 tells us that whatever we do, whether eating or drinking, we should do to the glory of God. The wine Jesus made from water at the Cana wedding was remarkably fine. In Paradise Restored, it is probably safe to believe that food will taste better than we have ever experienced in this Earth under the curse.

Will We Eat Meat?

Romans 5:12 tells us that "sin entered the world through one man, and death through sin." This suggests that there was neither animal death nor human death before the Fall.

In Genesis 9:3, after the Flood, God said to Noah, "Everything that lives and moves will be food for you. Just as I gave you the green plants, I now give you everything." This tells us that before the Flood, in sinless Eden, man did not eat animals. In the future Eden restored, it seems unlikely that man will eat them.

Revelation 21:4 says that "there will be no more death...or pain, for the old order of things has passed away." The verse does not say "no more *human* death."

Isaiah 25:6 does say that the Lord will prepare a feast of rich food for all peoples, "a banquet of aged wine – the best of meats and the finest of wines." The word "meats" here is "marrow," and probably is figurative, meaning the "choicest food."

The Biblical arguments against meat eating in the eternal state seem persuasive. It is possible God might provide meat in some way that does not involve animal suffering.

Since God will prepare the finest foods for us, there is little doubt that we will feel more gratified by the taste experiences in the New Earth than we have ever been on this fallen Earth. If we can make convincing meat substitutes in the laboratory (and scientists are now growing real meat *in vitro*[135]) there is no reason an omnipotent God might not make steaks grow on trees!

Will We Rest and Sleep?

God rested on the seventh day, the Sabbath, before sin entered the world. Hebrews 4:1-11 says that resting is a believer's reward, but that unbelievers will not enter into it.

Jesus said, "Come to me, all you who are weary...and I shall give you rest."[136]

Revelation 14:13 says that those who die in the Lord will rest from their labor, for their deeds will follow them.

We may safely conclude that one of the pleasures of Heaven is rest. But will we sleep? Presumably we would sleep only if we can be fatigued in Heaven. Is that possible?

Certainly. God never promises that there will be no needs in Heaven, simply that He will meet all of them in comfortable abundance. We may deplete resources, but God will renew them.

If God ordained rest, and sleep is profound rest, and if sleep is pleasurable to us, why would we not sleep in Heaven?

Will We Work?

In Genesis 2:15, God "took the man and put him in the Garden of Eden to work it and take care of it."

Work is pleasurable and good. God ordained work before sin entered the world. Work was not a result of the Curse. Rather, the Curse made work tedious and frustrating.

Genesis 3:17-19 says, "Cursed is the ground because of you; through painful toil you will eat of it all the days of your life. It will produce thorns and thistles for you, and you will eat the plants of the field. By the sweat of your brow you will eat your food."

God loves to work. In John 5:17, Jesus said, "My Father is always at His work to this very day, and I, too, am working."

"My food," Jesus said, "is to do the will of Him who sent me and to finish His work."[137]

Jesus worked in a carpenter's shop, walked through the countryside, went fishing, sailing, healed, and taught. Consider these verses on work:

"Having all that you need, you will abound in every good work."[138]

"Whatever you do, work at it with all your heart, as working for the Lord, not for men."[139]

"You call on a Father who judges each man's work impartially."[140]

Since God is a worker, since Adam worked before the Fall, and since God values our work, it is virtually certain we will work in Heaven. In fact, Jesus makes it clear we will have work to do with this statement:

"Well done, good and faithful servant; you have been faithful over a few things; I will make you ruler over many things. Enter into the joy of your Lord."[141]

We will work and enjoy working in Heaven.

Will We Have Homes?
In John 14:2, Jesus says, "In the house of My Father are many dwellings."

The Greek word for "house" here is *oikos*, which means residence or household. The Greek word for dwelling is *monai*, an abode or resting place. This word derives from the Greek word *meno*, which means to remain, to abide, to live, to endure.

In 2 Corinthians 5:1, the word *oikos* is used to refer both to our earthly body or "tent," and God's "house not made with hands, eternal in the heavens."

This means that God's kingdom has many places where we can securely remain.

However, this verse probably does not describe our dwelling in heaven, because the Bible explains that believers are God's house and are a living temple (and the Temple by definition is the house of God.)

The New Testament states:

"But Christ is faithful over God's house as a son. And we are his house if indeed we hold fast our confidence and our boasting in our hope."[142]

"What agreement has the temple of God with idols? For we are the temple of the living God; as God said, "I will make my dwelling among them and walk among them, and I will be their God, and they shall be my people."[143]

"Jesus answered him, "If anyone loves me, he will keep my word, and my Father will love him, and we will come to him and make our home with him."[144]

"You also, as living stones, are being built up as a spiritual house for a holy priesthood, to offer up spiritual sacrifices acceptable to God through Jesus Christ"[145]

So, the many dwelling places in John 14:2 are probably the many believers who make up the living stones of God's house. The place Jesus went to prepare for us, therefore, is not a place in heaven, but the place of the Holy Spirit in our heart, sent following the Cross, Resurrection, and Ascension.

An emperor is a king of kings. An empire is a collection of kingdoms. The kingdom of Heaven is the King of kings ruling over the secure households (the hearts) of all His people.

There is, however, other Scriptural evidence that we will have physical houses in the New Earth.

Isaiah 65:21 says, "They will build houses and dwell in them; they will plant vineyards and eat their fruit."

This image implies not merely apartments, but homes with land – our estates in the New Eden. The citizens of the New Earth will build and plant, eat and rest, as Adam and Eve and all their children ever have; but in the New Eden, we will inherit an estate God prepared for us and freely develop it for our pleasure and to the glory of God.

WHICH WAY WILL YOU GO?

You can know your eternal destiny for sure. The Apostle John wrote, "I write these things to you who believe in the name of the Son of God so that you may know that you have eternal life."[146]

Unfortunately, sin confuses us. "There is a way which seems right to a man, but its end is the way of death."[147]

Fortunately, the Bible makes our options clear:

"The wages of sin is death, but the gift of God is eternal life in Christ Jesus our Lord."[148]

"For God so loved the world that He gave His only begotten Son, that whoever believes in Him shall not perish, but have eternal life."[149]

"God made [Christ] who had no sin to be sin for us, so that in Him we might become the righteousness of God."[150]

"Salvation is found in no one else [but Jesus], for there is no other name under heaven given to men by which we must be saved."[151]

"For it is by grace you have been saved, through faith – and this not from yourselves, it is the gift of God – not by works, so that no one can boast."[152]

Just Deserts and Salvation

You may fear that you do not deserve to go to Heaven. You're absolutely right. You don't. Neither do I, nor does any human being. We are all sinners and deserve Hell. But the Bible plainly promises,

"If you confess with your mouth Jesus as Lord and believe in your heart that God raised Him from the dead, you will be saved."[153]

"If we confess our sins, He is faithful and just and will forgive us our sins and purify us from all unrighteousness."[154]

"He does not treat us as our sins deserve or repay us according to our iniquities...as far as the east is from the west, so far has He removed our transgressions from us."[155]

"Whoever is thirsty, let him come; and whoever wishes, let him take the free gift of the water of life."[156]

Wouldn't it be tragic if you read this study of Heaven and did not get to go there?

The Greatest Decision of All Time

Please take a quiet moment to pray. If you are saved, you do not need to pray this prayer. Jesus said you should be born again, not born again and again and again.

But if anyone has never prayed this prayer, feel free to offer it to God today. God's chosen people are the people who choose God.

If you have doubts, take heart, because Doubt is the Mother of Faith. Anyone who honestly doubts will honestly seek, and whoever seeks will find answers in Christ that satisfy mind, body, strength and soul.

Prayer

Father in Heaven, I confess that I am a sinner. Since You are perfect, and I am not, my presence in Heaven would make it imperfect. I know that Hell is my destiny unless You save me. I want You. I want eternal life with You and with all Your people. I want to be free of my sinful nature. I want to be all You created me to be.

I know, Jesus, You are the only begotten Son of God and *are* God. I know You lived a perfect life, died in my place, paid the price of my sins, and that You accept me because I humbly and gratefully accept You.

Holy Spirit, please enter my heart. Make me acceptable to God the Father. Guide me for the rest of my earthly life and forever. I surrender all to You, Jesus, my Savior, my Lord.

If you prayed that prayer for the first time, please tell someone who already is walking with the Lord and let him or her mentor you in your new walk with Jesus.

In Heaven they are rejoicing over you.

You have begun the greatest and happiest adventure of all time.

APPENDICES

KEY BIBLICAL CONCEPTS

There are several words that Christians often use without clearly understanding their roots. They are:

1. atonement
2. soul
3. spirit
4. eternal
5. grace
6. glorify
7. justify and
8. predestination

Understanding these words greatly clarifies the meaning of key Biblical passages.

Atonement

Atonement is a made-up English word meaning "at-one-ment," that is, becoming at one with the will of God. It occurs in William Tyndale's English translation of the Bible, but its original use may date back to the 1300s A.D. The word occurs only once in the New Testament.

The Hebrew equivalent word for this is כִּפֻּרִים, *kippurim*, from the verb (כפר) which means "covering."

The Bible teaches that man is sinful, God is holy, and that man must strive to regain the communion with God that God created man to enjoy before the Fall.

Soul and Spirit

We often use the word soul and spirit interchangeably, but the Bible makes a clear distinction between them, as in this verse:

"For the word of God is living and active, sharper than any two-edged sword, piercing to the division of soul and of spirit, of joints and of marrow, and discerning the thoughts and intentions of the heart."[157]

From this passage we can see the following dichotomies in the human make-up:

4. Soul vs. spirit
5. Joints vs. marrow
6. Thoughts vs. intentions of the heart

Since God's word can divide the soul (Greek ψυχή, *psyché*, meaning soul, life, or self) from the spirit (Greek πνεῦμα, *pneúma*, meaning wind, breath, or spirit), the soul and the spirit are not the same thing. The same thing cannot be divided from itself. However, soul and spirit are both part of each human being.

Similarly, joints are not the same thing as marrow, but they are both part of the human physical body, which is integral to the identity of each human being.

Similarly, thoughts are not the same as feelings (intentions of the heart), but every human has both.

In English, spirit comes from the Latin word, *spiritus*, which means "breath." The Latin word for soul is *animus*, which is where we derive the word animals – for creatures with souls (as opposed, for example, to trees).

The Bible's term for the Holy Spirit in Greek is Πνεῦμα Ἅγιον, *Pneuma Agion*, or "Holy Breath."

Why would the third Person of the Trinity be the "breath" of God and not the "soul" of God? Genesis 2:7 suggests the answer:

"The Lord God formed the man (קָדָא, *adam*, man) of dust (רְפָע, *apher*, dry earth) from the ground (אֲדָמָה, *adamah*, land, from the same word origin as *adam*, man) and breathed (חַפָּנ, *naphach*, to breathe, to blow) into his nostrils the breath (הָמָשְׁנ,

110

neshamah, breath, spirit) of life (חַי, *chai*, age), and the man became a living (חַי, *chai*, age) creature (נֶפֶשׁ, *nephesh*, being, creature, self".)

The Holy Spirit is that which endows creatures with life – literally, it inspires (in-spirits) them. When it does so, the creature becomes a living – in Hebrew terms, and ageing – being.

Paul said, "In him we live and move and have our being."[158]

Only when God's Spirit breathed life into Adam's God-created body did Adam become a *nephesh* – a person with a soul.

The Breath or Spirit of God is what animates both the soul and the body. Without the Holy Spirit, neither the soul nor the body can come into existence as a human.

When touched by God's Spirit, a creature – body and soul – becomes alive. When God withholds His Spirit, a creature – body and soul – dies (Psalm 104:29).

The infilling of the Holy Spirit is more than merely being alive – it is a greater awareness and abundance of life as the human temple becomes the dwelling place of God (Romans 8:9-11, 1 Corinthians 12:13, Ephesians 1:13, 1 John 4:13, Isaiah 63:11, John 14:17, Numbers 27:18, Acts 15:8).

By contrast, if a human rejects God's grace, God's Spirit may still keep him alive for the appointed duration of his life, but he may be indwelt by evil spirits, rather than by God's Holy Spirit (Matthew 12:45). Such a person is alive, but not abundantly alive. Jesus said, "I came that they may have life and have it abundantly." (John 10:10)

Humanity and Time

When God animated the dust and created Adam, Adam became not merely a *nephesh* – a person – but a "living" person. This word "living" in Hebrew means an *ageing* person. That is, God created humans to dwell in the stream of time just as he created fish to live in water. If one fish asks another, "How is the water?" the second will reply, *"What water?"* Water is as essential to living as a fish as time is to living as a human.

Prior to the entry of death into the world, ageing did not produce decay. In Heaven, there will be time and we will age – but we will not decay.

Time is the measurement of change. Ageing in Heaven will be a measure of how we change – growing eternally in knowledge, skills, and understanding of our infinite Creator. But the difference between ageing in Heaven and ageing on this fallen earth is that in Heaven, there will be no deterioration. We will grow, but not decline. And there will be no shortage of time; we will never run out of it.

In God's Image

In consisting of a mind, soul, and body (all eternal, although one, the body, temporarily dies), humans are created in God's image; like Him, they are a Trinity.

This is not to say that God's Trinity is identical to man's trinity – they are similar, not identical.

In God's Trinity

- the Father is *not* the Son, but *is* God;
- the Son is *not* the Holy Spirit, but *is* God; and
- the Holy Spirit is *not* the Father but *is* God.

In the trinity of the human being,

- the mind of man is *not* his soul, but *is* the man;
- the soul of man is *not* his body; but *is* the man, and
- the body is *not* the mind but *is* the man.

The human identity is complete only in this God-created human trinity. When deprived of the body through the door of death, humans are incomplete until reunited with their restored, immortal bodies in the final Heaven.

God's Trinity is a mystery and impossible to *comprehend* (wrap our minds around), but it is a mystery that we can comfortably *apprehend* (grasp).

For example, God talks to Himself and refers to Himself in the plural – "Let us make man in our Image."[159]

So do we humans. We say to ourselves, "Let's go!" We consider this normal, not schizophrenic.

We are three "whats" – mind, soul, and body – but one "who" – a uniquely individual human.

God is three "whats" – Father, Son, and Holy Spirit – and one "Who" – the uniquely indivisible God.

Eternal

In the New Testament, the word for eternal is αἰώνιος, *aiónios*. This Greek word derives from αἰών, *aión* (English eon), which means "age" or "duration of time."

In Matthew 12:32, Jesus says: "And whoever speaks a word against the Son of Man will be forgiven, but whoever speaks against the Holy Spirit will not be forgiven, either in this age (eon) or in the age (eon) to come."

These phrases are similar in Hebrew. The word עוֹלָם, *olam*, means "age." *HaOlam HaZeh* means "the age that is." *HaOlam HaBa* means "the age to come." Loosely, these terms mean *"this* world" and "the *next* world."

Jesus, the second man in history to be called a rabbi (after John the Baptist), was perfectly attuned to the Hebrew views about "this world and the next" that prevailed in his day – and that would prevail in the Mishnah, the Jewish "oral Torah," compiled by Yehudah haNasi (Judah the Prince; c. 165-220 A.D.).

Here's an example of the word *olam* in Genesis 9:12 (literally translated):

"And God said, 'This is the token of the covenant which I make between you and between me and between every living creature that is with you, unto age-long generations (*olam*).'"

The Bible tells us that this age will end (2 Peter 3:10). Therefore, God's rainbow Covenant is not perpetual in the sense of being never-ending, but it is *"olam"* in the sense of lasting as long as this age does.

Our English word, eternal, derives from Latin *aeternus*, which derives from *aevum*, which also means "age."

All these words therefore mean "age-long." They do not necessarily mean "everlasting" or "never-ending."

When Jesus says He will be with us till the end of the age (*aión*), He does not mean he will *not* be with us *after* the end of the age. But He will be with us all along our journey through this age, which is a finite journey. He will continue to be with us in the New Heaven and the New Earth – but He will not continue to be with the unsaved in the Lake of Fire.

So, the Biblical words often translated as "never-ending" or "everlasting" actually mean "age-enduring." In context, they may mean "never-ending" – if the age over which they endure never ends. But also, in context, they may mean "lasting as long as an age" – and if the age in view is one that ends, so the meaning is that the thing in view will last as long as the age does.

To understand the Bible reverently and accurately, we should prayerfully consider the *context* in which God places these words.

Perish

In New Testament Greek, this word perish is ἀπόλλυμι or *apóllimi*, which means to kill, destroy, die, or pass away.[160]

In Old Testament Hebrew, this word is אָבַד or *abad*, which means annihilate, be lost, broken, to corrupt, destroy, die, obliterate, perish, ruin, waste, or wipe.[161]

So, the word perish is not difficult to understand. It just means to die or cease to exist.

The thought-provoking Biblical idea is the contrast of "perish" with "eternal life."

"For God so loved the world, that he gave his only Son, that whoever believes in him should not perish but have eternal life."[162]

The Bible seems to suggest that eternal life equals *not perishing.* So eternal life seems never to end, but perishing, the alternative, means coming to an end.

This suggests that the saved never cease to exist but that the unsaved do cease to exist. However, it does not explain exactly *when* they cease to exist. The Bible definitely states that perishing does not equal escape from punishment, for example, in Hell.

But it is equally possible to understand the Bible as teaching that punishment in Hell may last forever or may last for a time and then end with the extinguishing of the lost soul.

Key Biblical examples of the use of the word perish are:

"I give them eternal life, and they will never perish, and no one will snatch them out of my hand."[163]

"No, I tell you; but unless you repent, you will all likewise perish."[164]

"For all who have sinned without the law will also perish without the law, and all who have sinned under the law will be judged by the law."[165]

Grace

The word for grace in New Testament Greek is χάρις, *cháris*[166] (a feminine noun from *xar-*, "favor, disposed to, inclined, favorable towards, leaning towards to share benefit). *Cháris* is used of the Lord's favor – freely extended to give Himself away to people (because He is "always leaning toward them").

Cháris ("grace") answers directly to the Hebrew term *Kaná*[167] ("grace, extension-toward").

Both words refer to God freely extending Himself (His favor, grace), reaching (inclining) to people because He is disposed to bless (be near) them.

Cháris is sometimes rendered "thanks" – the Italians say *grazie* and the Spanish say *gracias* – graces – to say thank you; but the core idea of the word "favor, grace" is "extension towards").

Thus, grace is the act of God doing showing us favor or kindness by reaching out to us.

A good depiction of grace is Jesus extending His hand to Peter and lifting him, as Peter was sinking beneath the stormy waves on the Sea of Galilee.

Glorify

Glorify comes from the Latin *gloria*, which means "fame or reputation," which comes from the New Testament Greek word δοξάζω,[168] *doxázo*, meaning to ascribe weight by recognizing real substance (value).

The word comes from δόξα,[169] *dóxa*, meaning "the exercise of personal opinion which determines value."

The words doctor, doctrine, and doxology derive from *dóxa*. A doctor exercises correct judgment. True doctrine is a true belief. False doctrine is a belief that is untrue. Doxology is the knowledge of doctrine – the knowledge of a belief – true or false, as the case may be.

The Hebrew cognate for *dóxa* is דָּבַ[170] *kabad*, meaning "to be heavy, weighty, or burdensome."

Thus, to give something *glory* in the Hebrew sense is to recognize its gravity – to ascribe a proper weight to it – to exercise a true opinion of it – to recognize its truth worth.

The image behind this Hebrew word is that of a balance scale. A balance scale has a balanced beam and two pans hanging from each end of the beam. You can place an object in one pan and a standard weight in the other pan. If one pan is higher or lower than the other, the object is not equal to the standard weight. If the pans balance at the same level, the object is equal to the standard weight. If we weigh God in the balance, figuratively, we find His weight, his gravity, his value, his glory – and, of course, the weight of all the world would be found wanting in comparison to the weight and value of God, so this is only a word picture.

So, "glorifying God" means valuing him for who he really is; deeming him worthy, ascribing to Him His true worth. "Giving glory to God" means acknowledging His true worth. "Becoming glorified" means being valued for who we really are, for our true worth.

So, glory does not really mean "splendor" or "radiance." It really means "worth."

The *glory* of a saved person in Heaven is the worthiness of a person in that state – that he is truly *blessed* because by accepting grace through faith, God has saved him. In an odd way, literally *glory* of a lost person in Hell is the value of a person in that state – none, because he is truly damned – worthless.

To *be* glorified, then, means to be properly weighed and evaluated – as worthy or worthless.

In common usage, we rarely think of the glory in a negative sense, because the word is used most often in the New Testament to describe the just reward of *saved* people or to describe the *perfect* character of God. So our habit is to understand glory as synonymous with great value or worth. But that is only the meaning of the word when placed in such a context.

Justify

The word justify comes from the New Testament Greek word δικαιόω,[171] *dikaióo*, meaning to justify.

The root of this word is δίκη,[172] *dike*, meaning justice, judgment, or punishment.

Thus, to justify something is not to defend it as just but to judge it justly.

Technically, to *justify* evil is not to *defend* it but to judge it for what it is – *wrong*. To justify evil is to condemn it.

To justify good is to judge it for what it is – *right*. To justify good is to *approve* of it.

So, when we say, "justification of sin," it is a somewhat imprecise use of language. The only way one can justify sin, properly speaking, is to condemn it, because that is the only just appraisal of sin.

Predestination

The word predestine comes from the New Testament Greek word προορίζω,[173] *proorízo*, meaning to mark out beforehand. To understand this word, it is helpful to understand its roots:

Pro – means beforehand.

The word ὁρίζω,[174] *hórizo*, means "I separate, mark off by boundaries; I determine, appoint, designate." *Hórizo* is the word from which we derive horizon – the limits of vision.

Thus, to *predetermine*, in Biblical terms, means to set limits in advance – or to use a Latin synonym "to design."

God's predetermination, in Biblical terms, means God's design. It does not mean God's choice of our every decision or ultimate destiny. It means what God intended us to be.

For example, God designed or predestined Adam to live sinlessly in Eden. This does not mean that God imposed this inescapable fate on Adam, because, obviously, Adam chose to reject God's original design.

Exegesis Using Precise Etymology

A passage often translated with laxity is Romans 8:29, 30:

"For those whom He foreknew He also **predestined** to be conformed to the image of His Son, in order that He might be the firstborn among many brothers. And those whom He **predestined** He also called, and those whom He called He also **justified**, and those whom He **justified** He also **glorified**."

This is often interpreted this way:

God knew in advance whom He had selected (predestined) to be saved (justified) and to have eternal life in Heaven (glorified).

But what the Greek words accurately say is:

Those whom God foreknew (**everyone**, for He knew all of us in our mother's wombs and from before the foundation of the world) He **designed** to be conformed to His Son. And those whom He had so designed (**everyone**) He also **called**. And those whom He called (**everyone**) he **justly judged,** and on those He justly judged he **placed an accurate value**.

So, this passage, often called "the Golden Chain of Salvation" is really about *both* salvation and condemnation. It is the description of the consequence of accepting or rejecting God's grace.

The passage has these key components:

- **Grace**: God **reaches out** to mankind
- **Design**: God **plans** mankind's redemption
- **Consequences**: **judgment** flows from accepting or rejecting God's grace
- **Verdict**: accepting or rejecting God's offer of salvation leads to one of two **just results:** salvation or condemnation.

BIBLIOGRAPHY AND RESOURCES

When writing on a subject so timeworn as the Bible, it is hard to be original, even when trying. I have heard hundreds of sermons and read hundreds of books and articles, that probably have, consciously or subconsciously, given rise to thoughts and phrases that have become part of my work. To the extent humanly possible, I give credit to those sources. But if thoughts and phrases have crept into my writing for which others deserve credit that, through human error, I have failed to ascribe, I sincerely beg their pardon and welcome the opportunity to correct my honest mistake and attribute to them all the recognition that is their due.

This reminds me of an anecdote about James Whistler, the American painter, and his friend, Oscar Wilde, the Irish author. Whistler made a brilliant remark. Wilde said:

"I wish I'd said that!"

Whistler replied:

"You will, Oscar. You will."

The fact remains that most of my studies have always been based on primary research and the interpretation of ancient documents, including the Bible, Josephus, Eusebius, Herodotus, and so on. Doing that is just what interests me most.

ABOUT THE AUTHOR

I grew up exposed to Christianity, but in my late teens I concluded that the Bible was a compilation of myths, and, compared to the *Mahabharata* and *Arabian Nights*, rather inferior ones at that. I felt too smart to be a Christian.

But, after traveling the world and diving deeply into the great religions, I grew tired of *seekers* after truth – I wanted to be a *finder* of it.

My family urged me to read the Bible and visit a Church. I did so gingerly. I visited a mega-Church in southern California with projected chorus lyrics on a big screen. With the unsophisticated tunes and dear, white-haired elders (like me today), I felt all we were missing was Mitch Miller's bouncing ball.

The pastor, however, preached salvation through Christ alone. He promised that if I would walk to the alter and repent before God in Jesus' name, I would receive the Holy Spirit.

I doubted him, but I was rational. Faith is the daughter of doubt. I had crossed the Himalayas and met the Dalai Lama and trekked through steaming Java jungles to a Sufi shrine; I could walk down this air-conditioned aisle and quickly prove or disprove the pastor's claim.

At the Altar, a light flickered on in my heart. I had been in the occasional midnight chant and attributed this sensation merely to ambience. But it lasted. It lasted until today and will last beyond the horizon of time. I was saved.

The problem was that my mind was far behind my heart. My "educated" brain possessed clear and convincing proofs that the Bible was philosophically and scientifically wrong. So, I began to devote my intellect to the task of dismantling the Bible.

To my ongoing humiliation, the battering rams of "enlightenment" kept splintering against the resilient gates of Scripture. Everywhere I turned – archaeology, paleontology, astronomy, history, physics, mathematics, and philosophy – the Bible proved right, and I proved wrong.

I burned with shame to think how many Christians I had "defeated" in debate and how smugly superior I had felt to them. How could God have any desire to love me, who had been such an arrogant fool?

The answer came when I found I could witness comfortably to Muslims, Hindus, Buddhists, and skeptics, because I was familiar with their positions.

In the summer of 2008, my Church asked me to teach an adult Sunday School for three Sundays. I was extremely nervous. I simply didn't know the Bible well enough to teach it.

During those first three Sunday lessons, I was bathed in sweat. By the third, I learned that no substitute teacher had been found – and I ended up teaching the Bible, verse by verse, repeatedly, from then until Sunday, May 29, 2016.

In the course of doing this, I grappled with every problem and seeming contradiction in the Bible that I could find. From apparent discrepancies in chronology and with science, to the arcane mystery of Solomon's Sea, I discovered, through 8,000 hours of research and teaching and 1,005 GB of writing original course material, answers to every problem.

I was blessed to have a class of devoted and highly educated adults. Among them were a trained and professional theologian, philosophers, educators, mathematicians, physical scientists, a rocket scientist (literally) and Bible students of many decades. They were of inestimable help in correcting and guiding me, as I presented and tested my lessons. As iron sharpens iron, so we sharpen each other.

This work presents some of those discoveries we made together.

1. The English Standard Version (ESV) of the Bible https://biblehub.com/esv/genesis/1.htm
2. The Works of Flavius Josephus https://www.biblestudytools.com/history/flavius-josephus
3. Church History by Eusebius http://www.newadvent.org/fathers/2501.htm
4. The Histories of Herodotus http://classics.mit.edu/Herodotus/history.html
5. The Histories of Tacitus http://classics.mit.edu/Tacitus/histories.html
6. The Extant Works of Sextus Julius Africanus http://www.newadvent.org/fathers/0614.htm
7. Justin Martyr, Dialogue with Trypho, the Jew http://www.earlychristianwritings.com/text/justinmartyr-dialoguetrypho.html
8. The Mishnah, Talmud, and other Jewish texts https://www.sefaria.org/texts
9. The Star of Bethlehem, Frederick E. Larson http://www.bethlehemstar.net
10. Starry Night Pro Software http://www.starrynight.com/
11. Kalendis Calendar Calculator http://individual.utoronto.ca/kalendis/kalendis.htm
12. "When Did Herod the Great Reign?" Andrew Steinmann, Novum Testamentum, Volume 51, Number 1, 2009, pp. 1-29

13. "Josephus Reexamined: Unraveling the
Twenty-Second Year of Tiberius,"
David W. Beyer, Chronos, Kairos,
Christos II, edited by E. Jerry Vardaman
(Macon: Mercer University Press, 1998)
ISBN 0-86554-582-0

BIBLE WORKS BY THE AUTHOR

In Amazon Paperback and or Kindle E-Book

1. *The History of Jesus – The Life and Times of the Son of Man*
2. *The History of Genesis – From Eden to Egypt*
3. *The History of Moses – The Man of God*
4. *The History of Joshua and the Judges – Israel's Coming to the Promised Land*
5. *The History of Saul, David and Solomon – Israel's First Three Kings*
6. *The History of Israel's Divided Kingdom – from Solomon to the Assyrian Conquest*
7. *The History of Judah Alone – from the Assyria Conquest to Babylon*
8. *The History of Judah Restored – from Babylon to Jesus*
9. *The History of the Prophet Daniel – Truth in Exile*
10. *The History of the Book of Revelation – Beyond the Veil*
11. *The History of the Acts of Jesus' Apostles*
12. *Biographies of Jesus' Apostles –Ambassadors in Chains*
13. *Yearning for Eden – All the Bible Teaches About Heaven*
14. *Understanding the Books or Ruth and Job – Morality, Suffering, and Justice*
15. *Is Calvinism Biblical? Weighed and Found Wanting*
16. *An Overview of Islam for Christians*
17. *Answers and Aids to Bible Questions, Puzzles and Problems*
18. *The Scriptural Chronology of the Bible: How God's Word Keeps Track of Itself*

-----

[1] 1 John 5:13
[2] Proverbs 14:12
[3] Romans 6:23
[4] *"In necessariis unitas, in dubiis libertas, in omnibus caritas."*
[5] Romans 8:28
[6] John 14:2-6
[7] Philippians 1:20
[8] Philippians 1:23
[9] 2 Corinthians 5:6
[10] 2 Corinthians 5:8
[11] Revelation 21:1-5
[12] 1 Corinthians 2:9
[13] 1 Corinthians 2:10
[14] Luke 15:10
[15] Hebrews 11:16
[16] Colossians 3:1
[17] John 8:44
[18] Revelation 13:6
[19] CIA World Fact Book
[20] http://abcnews.go.com/2020/Beliefs/story?id=1422658
[21] Matthew 7:13-14
[22] Romans 3:23
[23] Isaiah 59:2
[24] Habakkuk 1:13
[25] Revelation 21:27
[26] Luke 12:20
[27] Hebrews 9:27
[28] John 5:28-29
[29] Matthew 25:41
[30] Matthew 10:28
[31] Matthew 8:12
[32] Matthew 13:42
[33] Mark 9:48
[34] Luke 16:19-31
[35] Matthew 25:46
[36] Strong's Greek 622
[37] Strong's Hebrew 6
[38] John 3:16
[39] John 10:28
[40] Luke 13:5

[41] Romans 2:12
[42] Mark 9:48
[43] Strong's 5485
[44] Strong's 2580
[45] John 14:6
[46] Hebrews 2:14,15
[47] 1 Corinthians 15:55
[48] Jeremiah 29:11
[49] Revelation 21:1-4
[50] Revelation 22:1-5
[51] Hebrews 4:12
[52] Acts 17:28

[53] We call Evolution a Theory because it is an idea that has yet to be proven. We call Newton's ideas Laws because they are proven.

[54] Physics texts today insist that this Law applies only to an "isolated" system, not to any system. This idea of an "isolated system" was introduced after Newton. The reason is that if they remove the word "isolated," the Theory of Evolution collapses. Since modern scientists conclude, *a priori,* that their pet Theory of Evolution is true, they modify the Law to accommodate the Theory. They do not, as true scientists should do, reject the unproven Theory that a proven Law disqualifies. They reason like this: (a) since the Theory of Evolution is true, and (b) since the Law of Entropy would mean that Evolution would be untrue – that is, life would tend to become less organized and complex, rather than more organized and complex, (c) therefore the Law of Entropy is true only somewhere at some times, but not here and now. In other words, it's true throughout the universe – just not here on earth. What they should say is (a) the Law of Entropy is proven, (b) Evolution is an unproven Theory, (c) the Law of Entropy makes the Theory of Evolution impossible wherever the Law of Entropy applies, (d) the Law of Entropy applies throughout the universe, (e) the earth is in the universe, and thus (e) the Theory of Evolution is impossible on earth.

[55] Philippians 1:23

[56] The past and present of Heaven and Hell may not be qualitatively different, but our comprehension of them is more complete, in light of the Resurrection, than it was by the light of Abraham's faith or Moses' Law. That is to say, there are not necessarily three heavens and three hells, but one Heaven

and one Hell, each of which changes, just as the Earth changes. For example, we know God will one day destroy this Earth and make a New Earth, but we do not necessarily postulate two Earths in simultaneous existence. Even so, if to God all times are soon, it is philosophically possible to consider that Eden, so long ago lost, this present Earth, destined to be lost, and the New Earth, destined for eternal security, are simultaneously present realties to a transcendent God.

[57] Revelation 20:14, 15

[58] Ibid

[59] Galatians 4:26

[60] Some say the New Jerusalem remains suspended in mid-air, hovering over the New Earth. However, Revelation 21:2 does not say that the New Jerusalem stops descending. This idea may come from the assumption that Heaven and Earth must always be separate. But the separation of Heaven and Earth is unnatural.

[61] Genesis 3:8

[62] Luke 16:22-31

[63] Luke 23:43

[64] Philippians 1:23, 2 Corinthians 5:8

[65] Revelation 6:9-11

[66] Hebrews 9:27

[67] Revelation 2:26, 3:21

[68] Acts 7:55,56

[69] 2 Kings 6:17

[70] Genesis 3:24

[71] Numbers 22:24

[72] 1 Samuel 28:12

[73] Matthew 17:1

[74] John 20:19

[75] Acts 8:39

[76] Acts 4, 5, 12

[77] 2 Corinthians 12:2

[78] Revelation 4:1

[79] Isaiah 46:10

[80] Psalm 90:4, 2 Peter 3:8

[81] 2 Kings 2:11-12

[82] Luke 9:28-36

[83] John 5:28, 29

[84] Luke 15:7, 15:10

[85] Matthew 12:36, 37
[86] 1 Samuel 28:16-19
[87] Luke 9:31
[88] Romans 8:34
[89] Acts 9:4,5
[90] John 14:2-3
[91] Luke 9:12, Hebrews 11:14-16
[92] Hebrews 12:22, 13:14, Revelation 21:2
[93] *Source: Population Reference Bureau estimates.*
[94] Romans 2:14
[95] Matthew 7:23
[96] Revelation 21:12-13
[97] Revelation 21:11
[98] Revelation 22:1-2
[99] Revelation 22:2
[100] Hebrews 11:8-10
[101] Daniel 10:13
[102] Revelation 21:23
[103] Revelation 22:5
[104] Isaiah 60:19-20
[105] Genesis 1:3-5
[106] Genesis 1:16-19
[107] Genesis 2:19-20
[108] Isaiah 65:25
[109] Psalm 104:27-30
[110] Isaiah 65:17-25
[111] Isaiah 66:22-24
[112] 2 Peter 3:10-13
[113] Luke 24:39
[114] Romans 6:5
[115] Luke 24:39
[116] Job 19:26-27
[117] Matthew 8:11
[118] Matthew 22:32
[119] Luke 15:7
[120] Matthew 25:31-36
[121] 2 Corinthians 5:8
[122] 1 Corinthians 6:2-3
[123] Revelation 21:4
[124] Matthew 25:6
[125] Acts 23:9
[126] Galatians 5:22-25

[127] Galatians 5:19-21

[128] 1 Corinthians 13:4-8a

[129] 1 Corinthians 13:3

[130] Hebrews 11:1

[131] 1 Corinthians 13:12

[132132] Romans 8:24

[133] Revelation 2:7

[134] John 21:4-14

[135] http://www.reuters.com/article/2011/11/11/us-science-meat-f-idUSTRE7AA30020111111

[136] Matthew 11:28

[137] John 4:34

[138] 2 Corinthians 9:8

[139] Colossians 3:23

[140] 1 Peter 1:17

[141] Matthew 25:23

[142] Hebrews 3:6

[143] 2 Corinthians 6:16

[144] John 14:23

[145] 1 Peter 2:5

[146] 1 John 5:13

[147] Proverbs 14:12

[148] Romans 6:23

[149] John 3:16

[150] 2 Corinthians 5:21

[151] Acts 4:12

[152] Ephesians 2:8,9

[153] Romans 10:9

[154] 1 John 1:9

[155] Psalm 103:10-12

[156] Revelation 22:17

[157] Hebrews 4:12

[158] Acts 17:28

[159] Genesis 1:26

[160] Strong's Greek 622

[161] Strong's Hebrew 6

[162] John 3:16

[163] John 10:28

[164] Luke 13:5

[165] Romans 2:12

[166] Strong's 5485

[167] Strong's 2580

[168] Strong's 1391
[169] Strong's 1390
[170] Strong's 3513
[171] Strong's 1344
[172] Strong's 1349
[173] Strong's 4309
[174] Strong's 3724

Made in United States
North Haven, CT
03 December 2023

44972153R00093